imagine 01 – FAÇADES

Delft University of Technology, Faculty of Architecture,
Chair of Design of Constructions

imagine 01

SERIES EDITED BY
Ulrich Knaack
Tillmann Klein
Marcel Bilow

FAÇADES

Ulrich Knaack
Tillmann Klein
Marcel Bilow

010 Publishers, Rotterdam 2008

CONTENTS

chapter	page
INTRODUCTION – FUTURE FAÇADE PRINCIPLES	6
1. THEORY	10
FUTURE FAÇADE PRINCIPLES – THEORETICAL BACKGROUND	12
2. PROJECTS AND IDEAS	24
2.1. Concepts	26
2.2. Systems	48
2.3. Materials	84
2.4. Adaptables	108
APPENDIX	123
CVs	124
References	126
Credits	128

Imagine 01 FAÇADES

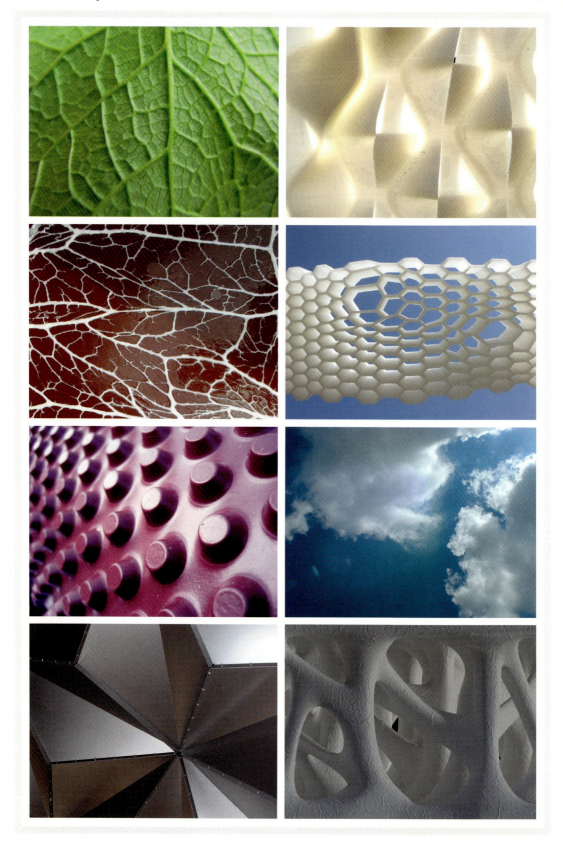

INTRODUCTION –
FUTURE FAÇADE PRINCIPLES

THE IDEA
Mike Davis, working for Richard Rogers on the Lloyds Building in London, proposed a "polyvalent wall": a system able to fulfill all the demands a façade poses. As early as in 1981 he mentioned photovoltaic, piezoelectric and photovoltaic technologies for parts of the façade, envisaging all these functions combined in a thin and layered solution. The result was well engineered, making optimum use of the technology available at the time, but it was neither layered nor thin – thus, the product was state-of-the-art, but did not provide a true solution to the initial goal. This was the starting point for our idea – how could we develop advanced façade technology and, at the same time, provide designers with ideas to realize their designs?

WHO
Within the Technical University of Delft / Faculty of Architecture, the Façade Research Group was set up as an impulse program to advance academic research in a field in which European engineering already is a world leader. The group is anchored within the Faculty, in the Building Technology department / Chair of Design of Constructions which is headed by Prof. Dr Ulrich Knaack.
Developing a program within a design faculty involves two aspects: adding to existing, but mainly project-driven research in a more strategically and academically oriented direction and, in parallel, establishing the idea of integration in façade technology – matching the demands upon and requirements of the envelope by using the more broadly oriented knowledge of architects in combination with the specialization of engineering disciplines. The starting point for the formation of the group was an analysis of existing strategic, technical and design-related knowledge, and of the different mechanisms of the market and established research. Then these results had to be linked. At present, several research projects and PhD theses are being studied – supported by universities and industrial partners. The PhD students Lidia Badarnah, Marcel Bilow, Thiemo Ebbert, Daan Rietbergen, and the researchers Ari Bergsma and Tillmann Klein, who also leads the research group, are currently involved in the program.
The group is linked to the "Material und Gebäudehülle" (Material and Building Cladding) research theme of the Detmolder Schule für Architektur und Innenarchitektur in Germany, where Ulrich Knaack holds the chair of "Entwerfen und Konstruieren" (Design and Construction), and also participates in the "Forschungsschwerpunkt Material und Gebäudehülle" (Material and Building Cladding specialist research) research group along with Marcel Bilow.

WHAT

Façade technology of the 20th century is related to the dissolution of the massive wall into a separation of structure and façade. Looking at the development of façade technology nowadays, after 60 years of curtain wall systems, 30 years of element-façade systems, and 10 years of experience with the integration of environmental services and double-skin façades, we must conclude that the peak of optimization has been reached. No further technological advance can be expected by continuing the policy of adding extra layers for each additional technical function.

In this book, the first in a series of IMAGINE books, we offer a collection of future principles for the façade. The collection provides a pool of ideas for architects, designers and engineers to deliver alternative viewpoints or consider new aspects. They are an offer of technology: public, for publication and use by others. The aim of the group is to expand possibilities, not hoard ideas – because, when stored away, they cannot be used for further developments and are consequently not worth the paper they are written on. The result ought to be a growing potential for façades or skin structures, principles, and methods of thinking. Stretching the limits of the possible is the mainspring behind all new development. And as long as the boundaries of the feasible have not been reached, we have not realized our full potential.

In combining different disciplines and technologies, we pursue the evolution of façades – or "skins", to apply a more relevant word – by using alternative, new and perhaps even embryonic technologies that have not been fully developed yet, but merely mentioned somewhere. The results are organized according to topic, and present the main idea by means of sketches, pictures and explanatory text. Keywords were used to organize the ideas in a database, and are highlighted in this book for quick orientation.

HOW

The prevailing approach to this research was to try to work with inspiration and an open mind. To achieve this, we needed not only an interesting and divers group of people who displayed mutual trust, but we also had to use various methods to create a supportive environment. Accordingly, several workshops with specifically prepared topics and rule-driven brainstorming sessions were held. In parallel, a variety of internal and external guests and a large number of students from both universities (Delft and Detmold) were prepared to support the program. We would like to make specific mention of Prof. Dr Holder Techen at the FH Frankfurt, Mathias Michel at University of Karlsruhe, and Thomas Auer from Transsolar / Stuttgart.

All material was developed as part of the "Future Façade Principles" program, or in courses and co-operative ventures linked to the program. We would like to thank all our colleagues and students for providing us with their materials, and especially Linda Hildebrand for her work in collecting the material for this publication.

Prof. Dr.-Ing. Ulrich Knaack

Imagine 01 INTRODUCTION

1. THEORY

Imagine 01 FAÇADES

1 Sao Paulo: Mega city Sao Paulo
2 New York: Mega city New York
3 Fish

FUTURE FAÇADE PRINCIPLES – THEORETICAL BACKGROUND

WHY?

The media provide us with information on the impact mankind is making on the earth and the resulting climate changes. Now, more than 30 years after the first investigations and conclusions drawn by the Club of Rome, we are finally concentrating a little more on the environmental impact of our behavior by focusing on energy consumption.[1]

This is particularly true when gasoline companies start branding their products by talking about research in solar cell farms, which only underlines the fact that energy is the most important aspect of and the driving force behind all developments. It is about trying to pass on to following generations an environment, which will give them a chance to survive without major troubles and a similar quality of life. So energy and the environmental impact on everything we do need to be evaluated, especially when 45% of the consumption is still related to buildings.[1, 2]

The second aspect is our changing society – meaning the transition from a goods-producing society to a knowledge-based society in which production is dominated by individualization and by speculation between those who produce and those who consume.[2] Knowing that this structure, still dominated by the Western world, mainly provides results and solutions for those able to pay, the belief in a change in the developmental expectations for the others is set. The result of this societal change is already evident in the ongoing globalization. In this context, we are not talking about prominent[3] brands or huge international companies – but more about the individual himself involved in this development: with friends in distant locations, communication via Skype, feeling lonely when the computer is turned off. The virtual world as part of our life has turned out to be quite different from what we expected.

A related aspect is the longing for individuality, be it as a nation, a society or even in personal partnerships. We express our status, education and goals via our choice of car or clothes we wear – trying to achieve maximum individualization. To support this trend, the knowledge-based society develops and provides strategies and tools for maximum result with, keeping energy in mind, minimal impact.

Finally – the quality. This book is authored by architects and engineers whose most prominent claim is that design quality makes life better. This is difficult to measure and at least as difficult to explain to community leaders not directly involved in the subject matter: some have a basic understanding of this aspect and expect good results; they might even expand on the concept by integrating control functions. One example is the Dutch system of setting up committees to judge and decide upon the design quality of architectural projects when building permission is sought. In other cases, the quality is controlled by finance, and it is up to the architect to determine how much design quality is realized and/or will survive the planning and building processes. But when looking at the so-called 'hard facts', the development of Swedish architecture can be taken as a contrary example: the building industry gradually appropriated more and more functions of the planning process, finally reducing architecture from design and process control to a function providing only schematic ideas. Even educational

4 Gothic Church – Amien
5 Fachwerkhaus Detmold
6 Federal Center Chicago
7 Stadttor Düsseldorf
8 Posttower Bonn
9 Schematic drawing of wall and façade development
10 The relationship between temperature and humidity influences the thermal comfort

programs were changed to accommodate this development – resulting in a limited delivery of outstanding architectural results. Nowadays, professional developers are striking back by requesting design quality – not only for the schematic design but also for the built result. Thus, universities are having to adapt their education to produce architects with design and construction qualities. The situation is driven by the financial world, not the academic one, meaning it must be a hard fact.

How do façades work? Of course, façade-building has a long tradition. Two main lines can be drawn – the massive construction, which we, after developing and building massive walls, initially tried to open up and then later closed again with glass, for energy-related reasons. During this period, the quality of the window increased and peaked in Gothic architecture with its somewhat undefined structural position. Now, can this still be regarded as a massive construction, or as a skeleton structure?

In parallel, the development of skeleton constructions can be observed – starting with simple tents, continuing with the European "Fachwerkhaus" (*half-timbered house*), and ending in modern balloon frame constructions. Related to these technologies, the separation of the main building structure and the façade started to occur. In building constructions, as in other disciplines, the separation between design and engineering was established in the 17th and 18th centuries. From this point on, design aspects can still be directly related to the construction, but are not necessarily so.

The separation of the skin from the structure in the development of the curtain wall, or the addition of a layer to the structure to envelop the building, became a characteristic feature of modern architecture. The next step was industrialization – initially used by architects more as an aesthetic approach than as a utilization of production technologies. This development is continuing with post-and-rail systems and element façades. In addition, the process of integration is advancing – with research in the field of climate control integration, where the façade becomes a part of the ventilation system within double-leafed façades and the latest development step of integrating service units into the façade itself, thus developing the entire system as a single industrialized product.[1]

INFLUENCES

Climate: the main function of a façade is the separation of the outside and inside climates to supply a certain quality to the enclosed volume. This sounds simple – however, this quality needs to be defined, and that is where the variations appear:

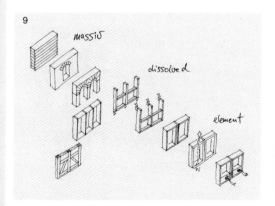

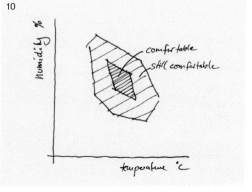

temperature in relation to humidity and ventilation. In addition, the façade has to provide protection against rain and wind as well as control the light.[3, 4]

Loads: wind and dead loads are factors that need to be taken into account in the construction. Loads may interfere with some demands posed by the climate: light / transparency can best be realized with a limited structural mass whereas the structural mass supports energy storage which can be applied to regulate the building temperature.[3, 5]

Materials: building materials have a long history – centuries of experience provide us with knowledge about the qualities of materials and the disadvantages related to the sustainability of some material constructions. As in any evolutionary process, good materials in good constructions tend to survive whereas less suitable ones disappear because they do not survive climate and usage requirements. Developments such as reinforced concrete have enabled major changes, greatly influencing architecture in terms of construction and design. New fields such as composite materials and nanotechnology are promising, but need further improvement in the evolutionary process.[6]

Production: even today – and we would have expected more development here – traditional craftsmanship and industrialized production processes exist side by side in building technology. In the field of industrial products, the prefabrication] of components is a hot topic. In addition, modular façades are in a state of advanced development. Comprehending the entire building as a single industrialized product does exist in theory, but not yet in practice.

One development that will influence this area in the future is directly related to the material itself: the process, energy for production, transport, assembly, disassembly, and reuse of the product. In view of the importance of energy consumption, a change in the evaluation of constructions is inevitable.

SYSTEMATIC THOUGHT AND DEVELOPMENT PROCESSES

Architecture is one of the last generalized disciplines based on broad knowledge but a limited amount of specialization. So it is about judging and integrating decision-influencing parameters. Architects see themselves as communicators and design-decision advisors. As a result of continuous developments in other disciplines, the knowledge base is growing exponentially. To control and steer the planning process, architects need to understand the basic principles of each discipline involved in a given project. One strategy employed to solve this issue is the separation of the problem from the solution. The division of labor into various segments is a broadly

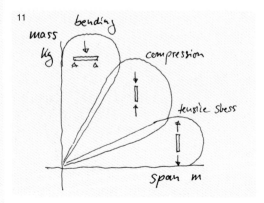

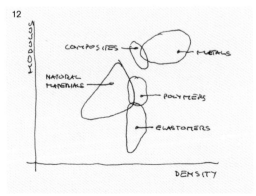

used method, typical of industrialized society. For construction, this means a division into structure, climate and design – and, of course, additional areas for specific aspects. Thus, current façades are developed in layers – resulting in a subdivision of the problems and a subdivision of the solutions. The obvious disadvantage is that some layers influence, react or interfere with other layers. The interesting aspect is that the current systematic approach of layering façade elements is coming to a developmental end. Subsequent developmental steps will only deliver small adjustments, compared to the amount of investment in knowledge and financing. A strategy to reorganize this process is the integration of knowledge right at the beginning of the design process by using parallel elements, for example. The next step could be the development of hybrid solutions – not merely a combination of components, but rather the combination of functions in all-serving components.[3, 7]

EVOLUTION PROCESSES IN THE BUILDING INDUSTRY

Compared to other disciplines, architecture and building construction are accused of being conservative – which may be partly their own fault. This could be largely due to our long experience in building with proven technologies and, as a result, the broad and continued acceptance of known technical and formal features. Moreover, related legislature remains conservative because of the expected risk and the typically long lifespan of a building. However, if we look at the developments in other disciplines involving long-term products or capital goods, we find that the development of a long-range airplane, for example, takes more then 20 years from idea to product. One difference with architectural products is that the production of airplanes needs a certain amount of payback for the research done – we expect about 80% of the construction to be the same and about 20% individualized – whereas a building is developed and built over 2-3 years.

Here, research works in an evolutionary way: individual research for each building adds to universal knowledge and thus broadens possibilities. A second aspect to consider is the accelerating rate of intellectual and technological developments: drawn on a timeline, the development of technology can be seen as an exponential graph, having led to a doubling of knowledge in half the time that was needed to double it previously.

With this in mind, this book is research-driven and tries to identify the next evolutionary steps, with a focus on the façade – or rather, the whole building envelope. This can be done by investigating the next

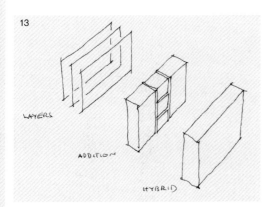

11 BIC diagram according to Frei Otto: load systems bending, compression or stress in relation to the mass needed for the structure
12 Modulus density diagram by Michael Ashby
13 Layered, additional or hybrid façade solutions
   See pages 18 - 21
14 Development of building technology in relation to historical developments, by Daan Rietbergen

Imagine 01 FAÇADES

Gaspard Monge, founder of the École Polytechnique, developed a graphic protocol which allows an imaginary object to be drawn so that it can be 3D modeled

The Jacquard Loom uses punched cards to govern the weaving of complex patterns. Joseph-Marie Jacquard was not the first one with the idea, but he perfected the work of his predecessors.

Printing Press
1436 - Johannes Gutenberg

Logarithms
1614

Cast glass process
1687 - Bernard Perrot

Improvements in iron
1740

Wedgwood
1759

Lithography
1798 - Alois Senefelder

Jacquard Loom
1801 automated weaving machine

Difference Engine

Portland Cement
1824 - Joseph Aspdin

Glass quality improves
1839 - Chance brothers improve the

1500 1600 1700 1710 1720 1730 1740 1750 1760 1770 1780 1890 **1800** 1810 1830 1830 1840 **1850**

Mainstream Architecture

1748 Rome, birth of the engineer. Giovanni Poleni draws up a report for the dome of St Peter's.

1748 Rome, birth of the engineer. Giovanni Poleni draws up a report for the dome of St Peter's.

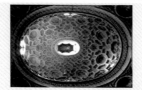

1779 Ironbridge (Severn Gorge) First iron structure in the world.

1838 Palm House (London)

AGE OF ENLIGHTMENT
SCIENTIFIC REVOLUTION
INDUSTRIAL REVO
30 Years' War
French Revolution
Napoleanic Wars

Imagine 01 **FUTURE FAÇADE PRINCIPLES**

In 1913 the assembly line for the Ford Motor Company opened representing super mass production.
In 1918 half of all cars in the United States was a Ford T.

Reinforced Concrete
1867

Linotype Machine
1883 - Ottmar Mergenthaler

Glass - Libbey-Owens process
1905 - Irving Colburn - Glass production more efficient

Offset Printing
1906 - Ira A. Rubel

Stainless steel
1911 - Leon Guillett

Glass architecture
1914 - Visionary book by Paul Scheerbart

Polyamide fibres (nylon)
1932

1870 1880 1890 **1900** 1905 **1910** 1915 **1920** 1925 **1930**

1851 Crystal Palace (Paxton)
An example of mass production during the Industrial revolution

1889 Eiffel Tower (Eiffel)

1891 Wainwright building, (Sullivan)

1903 Ingalls Building, Cincinatti

1911 Looshaus (Loos)

1929 Villa Savoye (Corbusier)

1886 Statue of Liberty (Bartholdi)

1900 Port Dauphine (Guimard)

1906 Casa Battlo (Gaudi)

1921 Einsteintower (Mendelsohn)

WW1

Imagine 01 **FAÇADES**

The Turing Machine, which is not a mechanical device but a thought experiment, is a very basic symbol-manipulating device which, by using algorithms, can be adapted to simulate the logic of any computer that could possibly be constructed.

The Intel 4004 originally designed for a calculator became popular for all kinds of applications.

Turing Machine 1936-37 - Alan Turing
First Digital Computer 1941 - First computer by Konrad Zuse
Finite Element Method 40's
Transistor 1947
CNC 1952 - CNC presented
Float Glass 1952 - Experiments started
Laser Printer 1969 - Xerox
Floppy Disk - 1971, by IBM
Intel 4004 1971 - First commercial microprocessor

1940 1945 **1950** 1955 **1960** 1965 **1970** 1975

Mainstream Architecture

1949 Glass House (Johnson)

1957 Centre Beaubourg (Nervi)

1967 Habitat 67 (Safdi)

1955 Notre Dame du Haut (Corbusier)

1962 TWA Terminal (Saarinen)

1973 Sydney Opera House

WW2 Korean War Vietnam War

Imagine 01 FUTURE FAÇADE PRINCIPLES

Although Personal Computers date back to 1972 this IBM 5150 is because of its popularity seen as the first personal computer.

WEB 2.0 represents the transition of websites from isolated information silos to web applications filled by the end users. WEB 2.0 decentralizes authority and is based on the freedom of sharing.

CAM
80's – connection CNC to CAD

Desktop Publishing
1985 – Apple LaserWriter

3D-Systems
1986

WikiWikiWeb

Evolution in materials
Evolution in mathematics
Evolution in form finding
Evolution in automated production

1985 — 1990 — 1995 — 2000 — 2005

eaubourg (Piano)

1985 Shanghai Bank (Foster)

1992 British Pavilion, Sevilla (Rogers)

1996 Educatorium, Utrecht (OMA)

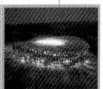
2008 National Stadium Beijing (Herzog & du Meuron)

taatsgalerie Stuttgart

1992 Vila Olimpica (Gehry)
The first structure completely constructed in CAD

1997 Guggenheim Bilbao (Gehry) Highly constructed using CAD/CAE

2001 British Museum (Foster)

2003 The amazing whale jaw (Nio)

DIGITAL REVOLUTION

Gulf — Iraq War

logical step in evolution and realizing it in solutions integrated in existing technology. Methods to achieve this can be fundamental, strategic, or process-oriented. With the increasing amount of knowledge, the complexity also increases whereas the number of individual steps taken decreases. Thus, the above-mentioned doubling of knowledge needs several times more research effort.

Alternatively, a new approach that can help us escape from this spiral is to start with a different technological idea, even if we have to accept that the result might not be as efficient as one produced by known technology. The advantage of this attitude is the possibility of developing new and future aspects to identify a fresh starting point for the evolution and, by doing so, ultimately a more efficient solution. Architects and product developers use this methodology in their design processes, aware that it initially seems like a step backwards. However, by learning about new possibilities, the increase in knowledge and the speed of subsequent developments will lead to better solutions.

A second strategy to develop knowledge is the assumption of possible results – the heuristic research method: drawing conclusions from existing facts and inspiring possible new solutions. In this case, we skip the research and evolutionary steps, and suggest possible results without yet knowing the technology required. Obviously, this strategy will lead to some possible and some impossible results. But it also provides the opportunity to combine unexpected results with the chance of unexpected routes in the development – both of which could be found with the investigative method as well, but in a slower process. Furthermore, the heuristic research method can lead to a new starting point for developments, which might deliver more promising solutions.

The ideas presented in this book are the result of this heuristic research method, exploiting the group's existing knowledge, imagination, inspiration and a certain amount of technical and aesthetical innocence, something seemingly counterproductive, yet, at times, highly valuable.

LITERATURE
1 Alex Steffen et al.: *World Changing – a user's guide for the 21st century*, Harry N. Abrams, Inc., New York 2006
2 Behnisch Architects, Transsolar Climate Engineering: *Ecology.Design.Synergy*, Berlin 2006
3 Ulrich Knaack, Tillmann Klein, Marcel Bilow, Thomas Auer: *Principles of Construction – Façades*, Birkhäuser Verlag, Berlin 2007
4 Klaus Daniels: *Gebäudetechnik – Ein Leitfaden fürArchitekten und Ingenieure*, Oldenbourg Verlag, Munich 1996
5 Frei Otto et al.: *Natürliche Konstruktionen*, Stuttgart 1982
6 Ashby Shercliff et al.: *Materials – engineering, science, processing and design*, Butterworth Heinemann, Oxford 2007
7 Gerhard Hausladen, Michael de Saldanha, Petra Liedl: *Clima Skin – Konzepte für Gebäudehüllen, die mit weniger Energie mehr leisten*, Callwey Verlag.

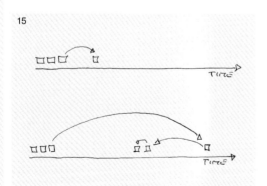

15

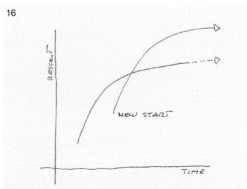

16

15 Evolution – the investigative and the heuristic strategy
16 Evolution in development processes
17 Evolutionary process in nature

2. PROJECTS AND IDEAS

ENERGY-FOR-FREE FAÇADE
TAKE YOUR HOME WITH YOU
FURNITURE ELEMENTS FOR FAÇADES
ONE-WAY HOUSE
LICHTENSTEIN ROOF SYSTEM
WASTE FAÇADES
INVISIBLE FAÇADE
PHOENIX FAÇADE
1 EURO FAÇADE
SEASONAL FAÇADE
RENT-A-PIECE-OF-MY-FAÇADE
LOW-TECH VENTILATION
LIQUID FAÇADE
CHANGEABLE ENVELOPE
LIQUID FAÇADE 2
GEQU ENERGY-COLLECTING ROBOTS
PROJECTIVE INSULATION
FUNCTION-INTEGRATED FAÇADE
INVISIBLE BUILDING
THE WOVEN ENVELOPE

2.1. CONCEPTS

Every solution begins with a concept. The idea is the starting point for progress: concepts are visionary thoughts, developed from a certain way of perception. They describe what the world could be like. Their task is to stimulate progress, although the initial idea might never be realized. The following ideas provide an extreme approach to solutions that are conceivable, yet far from realization. However, this can change over time and these ideas might be taken into consideration.

This chapter contains a deviant line of reasoning. It is about observing from a different point of view, about defining new ways to approach a problem by reversing it. Why not use the waste we produce to create a high-tech façade? New approaches are needed to face today's challenges.

Environmental and social aspects must be qualified: independently evaluated and freed from currently used methods and though processes. Changing user behavior results in changing requirements, which in turn lead to new possibilities. The façade can contain more functions to cope with and accommodate the speed of our times. This chapter is a compilation of visionary, sometimes extreme and adventurous ideas, based on an approach of encouragement, inspiration and imagination.

ENERGY-FOR-FREE FAÇADE
11-06-2007

IMAGINED BY Ulrich Knaack
KEYWORDS light construction, geothermal heat, vision

This idea contains a new and audacious approach. Why not invert the idea of a façade? Soil, in combination with a pump, can generate an adequate climate in buildings during winter and summer. Contrary to traditional efforts to decrease thermal conduction, this façade's only function is to protect against rain and wind. Air-conditioning inside the building is provided by the exchange pump. The idea is to use as much effort as necessary to fill the building's interior space with the quantity and quality required.

TAKE YOUR HOME WITH YOU
13-03-2006

IMAGINED BY Wiglinghoff
SUPPORTED BY Ulrich Knaack
KEYWORDS pneumatic, prefabricated, freeform, mobile, lightness, transport, textile, foil, membrane
WEBSITE www.studioorta.free.fr

A rope is a tent is your home.... Using combinations of textiles and structural pneumatic bars, you can handle and carry your own small room or tent when traveling. Everything you need is in the coat; thus, it could also be described as "coating" when looking at it from a general point of view....

FURNITURE ELEMENTS FOR FAÇADES
08-05-2006

IMAGINED BY Ulrich Knaack, Marcel Bilow
KEYWORDS prefabricated, decentralized, modular, system, mobile, adaptable, façade, interior, installations

Just like modular façade components, furniture elements are designed to fit into the façade grid. These elements can include tables, cupboards, beds, or showers. Prefabricated, just like the airplane door shown below, such elements can easily be realized in different styles and designs. Different materials are also possible. To achieve ease of assembly and a wider range of options, the goal would be to use a regulated grid, comparable to the iPod standard connection. There are more than 1,000 components that can be connected to this device. The modules might also be mobile, so that the user can carry them as personal equipment and use as part of a living unit.

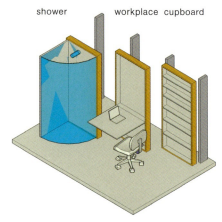

ONE-WAY HOUSE
11-06-2007

IMAGINED BY Ulrich Knaack
KEYWORDS individuality, one-way, deflateables, vision

Take your house with you and set it up wherever you like! Enter your customized user data, open your suitcase and a perfect temporary home appears – suitable for each environment and tailored to your individual needs. After a good night's sleep, the envelope with its casing can be thrown away.

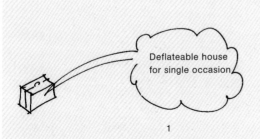
1

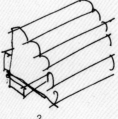
2

3

LICHTENSTEIN ROOF SYSTEM
29-08-2007

IMAGINED BY Guilherme Moretzsohn
SUPPORTED BY Ulrich Knaack, Marcel Bilow
KEYWORDS modular, interactive, adaptable, roof, plastics

Due to Google Earth's ongoing success, a new avenue for advertisement could be established. Using the Lichtenstein pixel phenomenon – which produces images that are created from individual dots and are clearly visible from far away – we could try to realize a roof system made up of boxes. A set of colored films rolled up in a supporting box can change the visible color of the roof. Depending on the distance of the viewpoint, this box grid could measure up to 1m x 1m. The idea exploits the latest feature of Google Earth; providing almost live satellite images. If the images can be updated in regular, relatively short and predictable intervals, advertisement can be placed on specific locations for specific time periods.

WASTE FAÇADES
08-05-2006

IMAGINED BY Ulrich Knaack
KEYWORDS freeform, economy, low-cost, façade, unknown material

This is a recycling idea: find otherwise unusable waste and use it for a façade construction.

INVISIBLE FAÇADE
22-02-2006

IMAGINED BY Tillmann Klein
KEYWORDS freeform, lighting, transparency, adaptable, façade, envelope, technology transfer, tool, vision, unknown material

Scientist have recently discovered how light reacts with solid matter. They already developed a special material that becomes transparent when hit by laser beams. This opens up new possibilities for building materials. Massive load-bearing structures can be made invisible by using a switch that turns the laser on. The transparent or 'open' areas can have any desired shape and can change continuously. The problem of sun-shading is solved. The invisible façade is a façade made out of one multi-purpose material.

PHYSIK
Röntgenblick per Laser

Durch Wände zu sehen ist einzig eine Frage des richtigen Lichts. Zu diesem verblüffenden Ergebnis kommt eine Forschergruppe um Chris Phillips vom Imperial College London im Fachmagazin „Nature Materials". Die Physiker schufen im Labor ein Spezialmaterial aus winzigen Kristallen. Mit einem Laser beschossen, wird das normalerweise undurchsichtige Material wie von Zauberhand lichtdurchlässig. „Es entsteht ein rundes Fenster, durch das man hindurchsehen kann", berichtet Phillips. Der Trick funktioniert, weil sich die Lichtwellen des Lasers und die Elektronen des Materials ähnlich wie zwei Wellen auf dem Wasser gegenseitig beeinflussen können. Noch lässt sich der Effekt nur bei Spezialmaterial erreichen. Phillips hält es jedoch nur für eine Frage der Zeit, bis der „Röntgenblick" auch normale Türen oder Mauern durchdringen wird: „Wir beginnen zu verstehen, wie Licht mit fester Materie interagiert", sagt Phillips. „Auf Basis dieses Wissens wird es künftig möglich sein, Speziallaser zu entwickeln, die eine Vielzahl von Materialien lichtdurchlässig machen können."

Physiker Phillips

138   DER SPIEGEL 9/2006

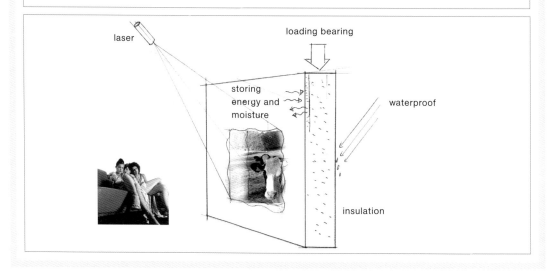

PHOENIX FAÇADE
07-09-2007

IMAGINED BY Daan Rietbergen
KEYWORDS refurbishment

Kurt Cobain and Coop Himmelb(l)au both told us; *'It's better to burn out then to fade away'* (Kurt Cobain) and *'Architecture must burn'* (Coop Himmelb(l)au). So let's make a building that auto-destructs in a spectacular blaze every few years and reconstructs itself into a new building. Though the Phoenix is said to have lived for 500, 1,461 or 12,594 years (depending on the source), most buildings don't survive more than 50 years, usually less. After its useful time serving our communities, the building is an unwanted obstacle annoying its occupants. By developing a façade, which ignites itself when it feels unwanted, we would not only obtain a beautiful new building, but would also be able to dispose of all annoying occupants. The technology behind such a façade would be very tricky. A combination of combustible materials and incombustible technology would need to be invented. The combusting material should, once the fire is dowsed, continue its reaction to rearrange itself into a new, combustible material.

1 EURO FAÇADE
18-04-2006

IMAGINED BY Tillmann Klein
KEYWORDS modular, system, commercial, low-cost, façade, envelope, 0-1 years, unknown material

The cost factor is becoming increasingly important in façade constructions. But what happens if costs become the dominating factor in the design discussion? How far can we realize a low-cost façade and what performance can we expect? Is it our limited imagination or fixed claims about façade functions that drive us to build the façades we have always built? The 1 Euro façade is an experiment. The rules have to be defined and set before the game begins.

Scenario
Step 1   Research in absolute basic façade requirements (functions, climate, protection, loads, etc.).
Step 2   Definition of design goal (user type, local climate, type of building, etc.).
Step 3   Find materials and strategies, and combine them using brainstorming sessions.
Step 4   Evaluation and mock-ups.,

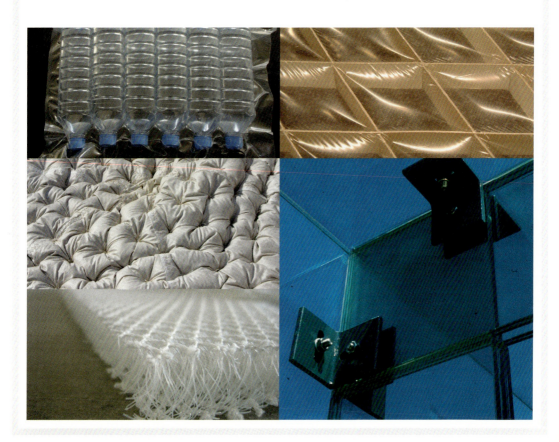

SEASONAL FAÇADE
20-08-2007

IMAGINED BY Arie Bergsma, Marcel Bilow, Thiemo Ebbert, Tillmann Klein, Ulrich Knaack, Raymond Van Sabben, Lidia Badarnah, Daan Rietbergen, Holger Techen, Matthias Michel
KEYWORDS summer/winter, season, chemical, movement

This double-glazed façade contains some kind of advanced material that changes its state from season to season. In the summer, it forms into the shape of clouds to shade the interior. In the winter this advanced material reacts with another substance in the façade, to make the clouds disappear and let light permeate through the façade and heat the interior.

RENT-A-PIECE-OF-MY-FAÇADE
19-04-2006

IMAGINED BY Daan Rietbergen
KEYWORDS interactivity, media

A building is covered by a grid of pixels. The pixels can be rented out in small parcels for certain time periods. These parcels can be used for any purpose: personal messages, art, advertisements, gaming.

LOW-TECH VENTILATION
10-04-2006

IMAGINED BY Marcel Bilow
KEYWORDS economy, security, ventilation, controlling, low-cost, tool

Ventilation is very important for user comfort and health. However, if you open the windows for extended periods of time, any energy-savings will be lost. The idea is to create a smart sensor attached to the façade or the walls, equipped with an optical signal that indicates when the carbon-dioxide level rises above a certain value, meaning you should ventilate by opening the window. When it deceases, you can close the window again. There are solutions that make use of electrical components; the better ones should react without electrical energy, similar to the thermometers attached to wine bottles.

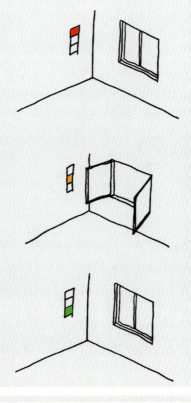

LIQUID FAÇADE
13-03-2006

IMAGINED BY Ulrich Knaack
KEYWORDS pneumatic, controlling, liquid, façade, foil, water

The liquid façade tries to deal with the following factors: load-bearing, thermal mass for energy storage, and different possibilities of thermal insulation. By filling the middle pneumatic element with water, the thermal mass can be used to store energy. By varying the positions of the insulating pneumatics on the outer surface, the insulation properties against the sun and the cold can be controlled.

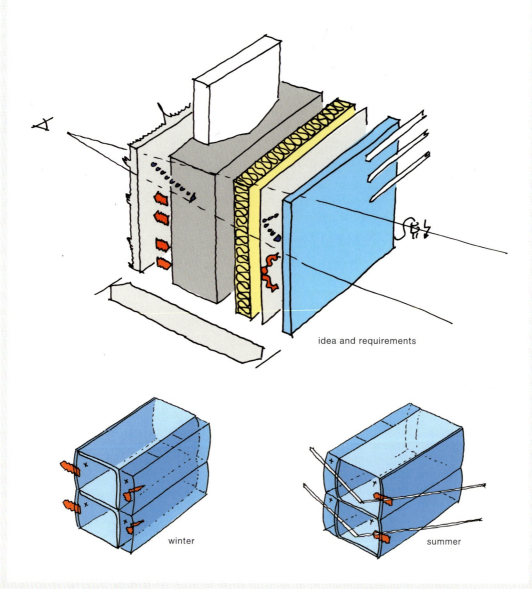

idea and requirements

winter   summer

CHANGEABLE ENVELOPE
13-03-2006

IMAGINED BY Ulrich Knaack
KEYWORDS pneumatic, energy generation, liquid, envelope, glass, foil

The changeable envelope relates to semi-permeable and three-dimensional fabrics. This provides the possibility of integrating humidity control in closed surfaces. In addition, the principles of vacuum and pneumatics could be used to regulate the functions of the envelope.

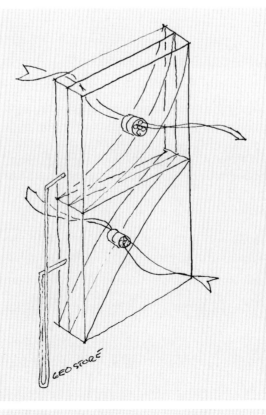

LIQUID FAÇADE 2
01-07-2007

IMAGINED BY Arie Bergsma, Tillmann Klein, Ulrich Knaack
KEY WORDS liquid façade, energy performance, climate control

The idea is to create a climate-adaptive façade – with liquid materials used as the media to vary the building-physical properties of the façade such as thermal insulation, incidence of daylight, solar shading, etc., and to cool and heat the building. The solution should focus on the symbiosis of different properties in one material. One could, for instance, think of a system of multi-layered cushions (such as Lexan panels) with different compartments, which can be filled and refilled separately and independently of one another: either with water, air, or other liquid material. Dynamic climate-controlled façades that can adapt their building-physical properties to the changes in the outdoor climate that occur with the time of day and season as well as make optimum use of the collection of solar energy can play an important role in improving the energy performance of future buildings and the interior climate.

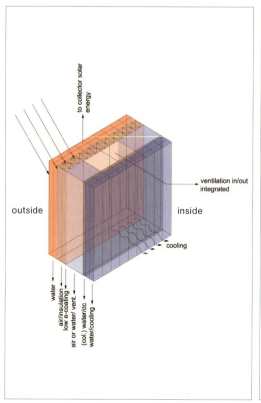
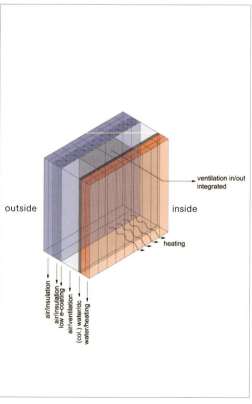

GEQU ENERGY-COLLECTING ROBOTS
29-08-2007

IMAGINED BY Heike Lau
SUPPORTED BY Ulrich Knaack, Marcel Bilow
KEYWORDS modular, interactive, adaptable, roof, plastics

The idea of the GeQu is based on the principle of a group of consuming and producing animals, like a herd of cows, which collects energy by eating grass and produces milk as a result of this activity. Our herd of energy-collecting animals is a group of self-walking and climbing robots that employ the principle of the Van der Waals force – the method by means of which a gecko sticks to the wall. The robot itself is covered with PV cells to convert solar energy into electricity.
A variant with a decentralized climate unit is also conceivable: for renting out single climate units for example. A sun-shading device could be realized by using translucent PV elements, depending on the number of robots per square meter. The group of GeQus moves during the daytime according to the position of the sun. This idea could also be used to produce rental units – click and order a set over the internet.

PROJECTIVE INSULATION
07-09-2007

IMAGINED BY Lidia Badarnah, Daan Rietbergen
KEYWORDS insulation, lightness, transparency

The myth about how the polar bear stays warm is that the skin is covered by hollow light-transmitting (fiber-optic) fibers, its fur. This was supposed to be the reason why the polar bear's skin is black. Even though there are recent studies that disprove this theory, let's develop such an insulating material ourselves! Optical fibers project an image on the inner façade. As the wind flows through the fibers, the image gently transforms.

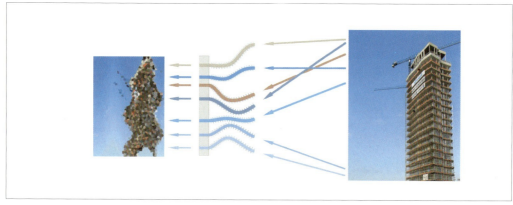

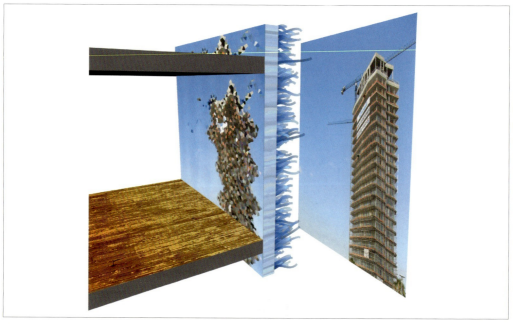

› Imagine 01 CONCEPTS

FUNCTION-INTEGRATED FAÇADE
07-11-2007

IMAGINED BY Marcel Bilow, Ulrich Knaack, Jens Böke
KEYWORDS function integration, force-following structures

Function integration for façades means developing structures that can bear loads as well as accommodate service units for ventilation and conditioning. Rapid prototyping technologies provide the possibility to develop this idea into completely integrated units.

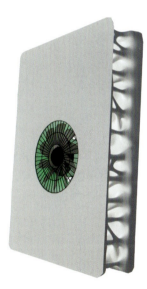

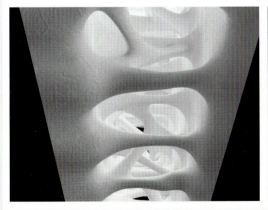

INVISIBLE BUILDING
20-08-2007

IMAGINED BY Lidia Badarnah
KEYWORDS fly's eye, invisible, bio-inspired, light, optic fibers.

The façade is like the eye of a fly. It is covered with a large quantity of small lenses on either side, with optical fibers attached to the lenses. The light enters on one side and is transferred through the optical fibers to the other side. By doing so, we transfer the image from one side to the other.

A large amount of small lenses covers the interior and exterior side of the façade to project the image on either side to the other side

THE WOVEN ENVELOPE
18-04-2006

IMAGINED BY AR0645
SUPPORTED BY Lidia Badarnah, Daan Rietbergen
KEYWORDS layered construction, ventilation, insulation, sun shading, mobile, beauty, façade, 10-20 years, textile

High performance textiles. Building envelopes like cloth. The beauty of woven materials. The term "Curtain wall" takes on a new meaning on a different level. Textiles can be layered. They can be tailor-made, they can adjust their form. Ventilation and waterproofing can be achieved simultaneously.

Scenario
Research about textiles in general. Weaving methods, weaving structures, and the combination of plastics and fibers. How can façade functions be realized with textiles? Layering, structure, load-bearing, ventilation, vision, etc. What are the specific opportunities textiles offer for façade construction? Mock-ups, models, drawings….

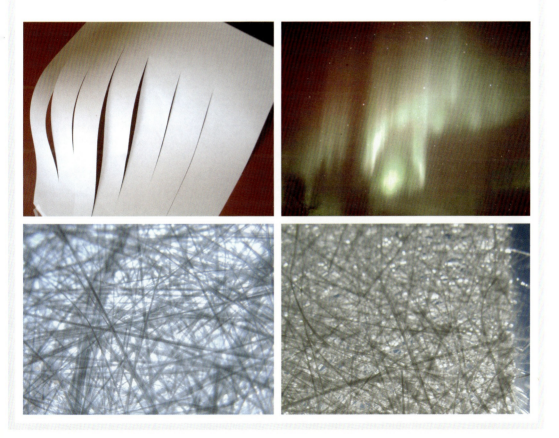

INTEGRATED MODULE FAÇADE
POLAR FILTER
CREATE YOUR SKIN
SOLAR ENERGY
PNEUMATIC STRUCTURES
FEATHER ENVELOPE
FOLIAGE FAÇADES
CAMEL FAÇADE
DESERT BEAR
REVOLVING COLLECTOR
HAIR-PROTECTED FAÇADE
SHADING VENTILATION FAÇADE
SKINNY FAÇADE
REFLECTION FAÇADE
SPONGE FAÇADE
SPONGE RUBBER FAÇADE
FAÇADE HEATING / COOLING PANEL
ADAPTRONIC WINDOW HANDLE
FUNARIA HYGROMETRICA - IRIS DIAPHRAGM
FAÇADE SERVICE SLOT
FLEXIBLE TEXTILE WINDOW / GILL FAÇADE
SELF-EXPANDING LINEAR JOINT
GLUED TEMPORARY CONSTRUCTION
PLUG AND PLAY
ENERGY STORING BRICK
BOTTLE CASE FAÇADE
(RE)FOLDABLES
(RE)FOLDABLE PAVILION
(RE)FOLDABLE EXHIBITION WALL
INTERWOVEN TEXTILE FAÇADE
FIBER-CONCRETE FAÇADE POSTS
SNAKESKIN

2.2. SYSTEMS

Some fabrics are able to reflect infrared beams, reduce the wind pressure by offering less friction, and also let sweat permeate without spending any energy. At present, no façade is able to work like this. This chapter is about showing existing solutions and how they are transferable to a façade system in order to improve technology and effectiveness. It focuses on existing solutions in other disciplines, looks at the procedure in order to extract the principle and applies them in building devices. Nature and technique – like birds and the building industry – have to deal with the same difficulties. Both have to face air resistance, temperature differences between the inside and outside, etc. Why not use layers of feathers to insulate a building?
The following section contains not only natural and evolution-based solutions to problems: diverse scientific disciplines have discovered mechanisms and materials that make new procedures conceivable.
The textile industry has invented fabrics with a huge range of abilities. They can be produced with individual qualities such as transparency, color, air permeability and humidity.
To reduce the façade's features to an efficient system with individual qualities is a vision that has not yet been realized, but nevertheless is getting closer with the transfer of knowledge. The following principles give no exact description of the procedure but present transferred working systems in order to invent solutions which may work in the medium term. The shown solutions are regarded with a different approach – one preceding existing technologies.

INTEGRATED MODULE FAÇADE
28-06-2006

IMAGINED BY Ulrich Knaack, Marcel Bilow
KEYWORDS decentralized, heating cooling, transparency, installations, façade, concrete

The aim of this prototype project is to add new functions into a façade module. A decentralized climate unit is inserted into the façade frame, and a cable duct for data transfer and electric power to the office is added to the system.

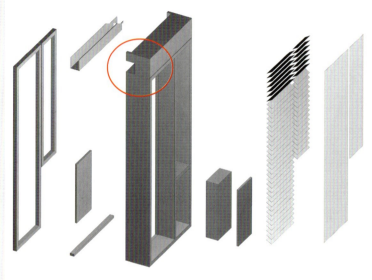

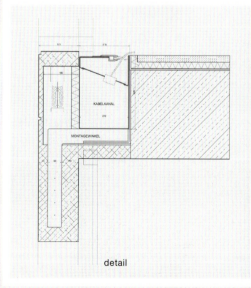

detail

POLAR FILTER FAÇADE
29-08-2007

IMAGINED BY Marcel Bilow
ELABORATED BY Daniel Kräft
KEYWORDS modular, sun shading, adaptable, envelope, glass

Two layered, polarized filters can be used to regulate visibility by rotating one of the filters against the other. If one applies this principle to a window, the system must be arranged in circular shape. The function of ventilation could be realized with hydraulic cylinders, allowing the window to be opened in different positions. The polarized filter principle can be applied in window size or by using a series of small filters, each with a diameter of a few centimeters.

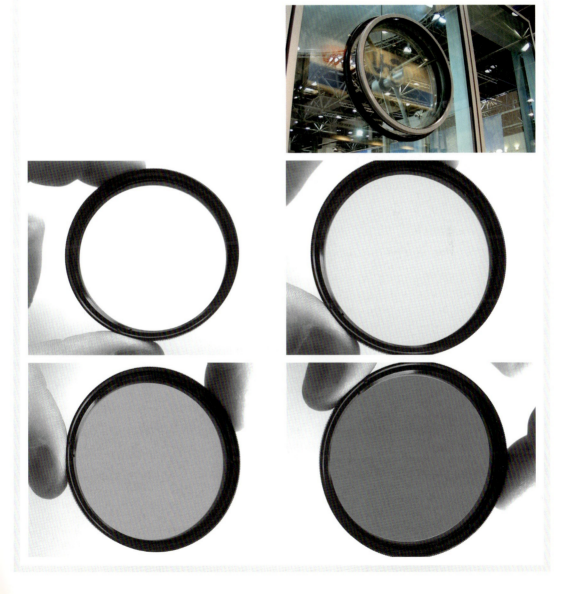

CREATE YOUR SKIN
15-08-2006

IMAGINED BY Marcel Bilow
KEYWORDS freeform, mobile, adaptable, adjustable mold, foil

A custom-made, flexible skin can be made from fibers or ropes and liquid latex. The direction of the tensile force elements in the rubber matrix is free, providing the option of creating a skin that can be formed into any desired shape to accommodate any need.

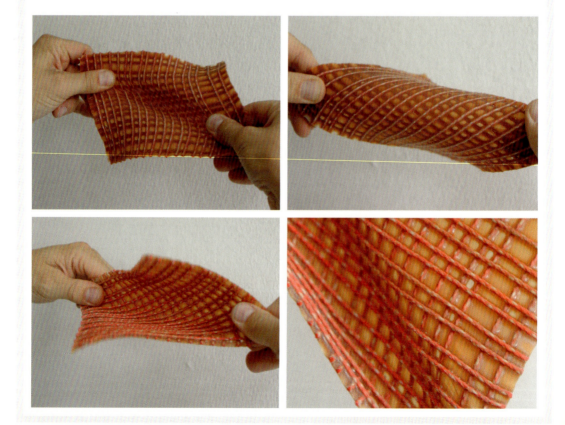

SOLAR ENERGY PLANT
13-03-2006

IMAGINED BY Marcel Bilow
KEYWORDS layered construction, composite, modular, energy generating, load-bearing, strength, façade, envelope, textile, concrete, 3-D fabrics, composite

The idea is to create collectors in areas that are typically used for traditional solutions. Walls or roofs can be used as solar energy plants with inserted capillary tube systems, so that the function of solar energy input can be added to the functions of load-bearing, insulation and weather protection. The material is fiber-reinforced concrete. The idea is geared toward industrial roofs or façades as well as prefab roofs for housing. A geothermic storage space seems possible to store the energy.

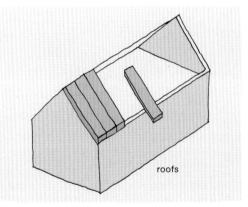

roofs

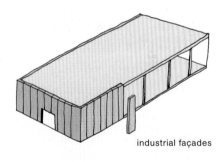

industrial façades

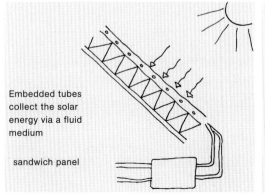

Embedded tubes collect the solar energy via a fluid medium

sandwich panel

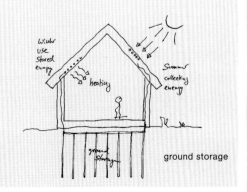

ground storage

PNEUMATIC STRUCTURES – SAND DOME
13-03-2006

IMAGINED BY Schütte, Sander
SUPPORTED BY Ulrich Knaack
KEYWORDS layered construction, pneumatic, insulation, load-bearing, low-cost, envelope, structure, textile

The idea for this façade is to use the possibility of the thermal mass of sand for tent structures in the desert. By mixing air and sand, sand could be use as a liquid, transportable material. In this design, the structure should be dome-shaped to provide maximum space with a minimum of surface area.

Imagine 01 SYSTEMS

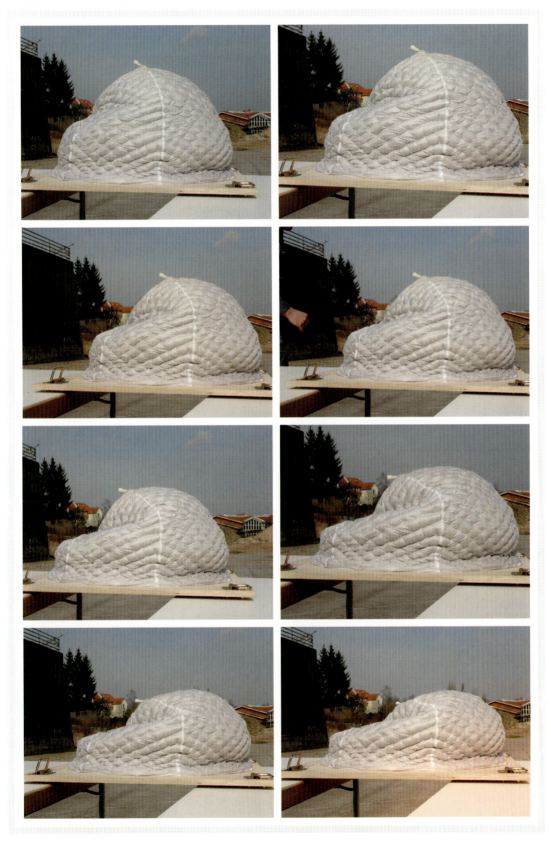

FEATHER ENVELOPE
15-05-2006

IMAGINED BY Tillmann Klein
KEYWORDS freeform, layered construction, ventilation, insulation, mobile, organic, beauty, façade, envelope, building physics, technology transfer, 10-20 years, unknown material

Houses could be covered with feathers. Feathers provide a watertight and insulating surface, which also complies witth any movement and is porous for ventilation if needed. In nature, there are two types of feathers: contour feathers form the outer layer. They are strong and are used for steering and protection. Down feathers are finer and serve as insulation. The part of the feather's shaft just above the skin is called hollow shaft or quill. It carries the vane, which itself is divided into air-filled barbs. The barbs and smaller barbules have minute hooks for cross-attachment to provide connectivity and strength. The feathers also protect against water. Blue colors are created by distribution of light. Green and violet are created by yellow or red layers on top. Changing colors come from interferences with white light.

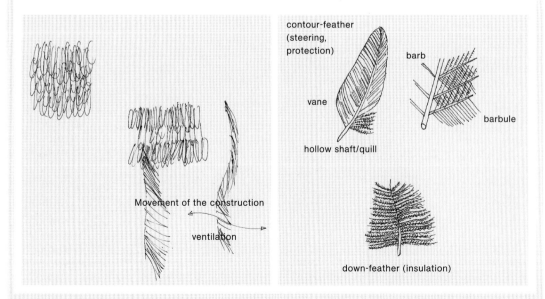

Imagine 01 SYSTEMS

FOLIAGE FAÇADES
08-05-2006

IMAGINED BY Ulrich Knaack
KEYWORDS bionic, energy generating, sun-shading, transparency, adaptable, organic, façade, glass

Integrating fern or foliage from other deciduous plants into the space between two glass panes will function as periodic sun shading. In winter, the plant has shed its foliage and lets the sun penetrate, but in summer there is good shading. The elements have to fill a reservoir with rainwater to let the plants grow.

CAMEL FAÇADE
19-05-2006

IMAGINED BY Linda Hildebrand
SUPPORTED BY Ulrich Knaack, Marcel Bilow
KEYWORDS reflection, insulation coating

Not only its complex water-storage system, high blood temperature and other systems for cooling, but also its coat protects the camel against overheating and dehydration. The fur's bright color reflects most of the sunlight. Additionally, the fur coat functions as insulation against the heat during the day and the cold during the night.

DESERT BEAR
22-05-2006

IMAGINED BY Linda Hildebrand
SUPPORTED BY Ulrich Knaack, Marcel Bilow
KEYWORDS guiding sunlight, directed energy effort

Even though this theory has been questioned in recent studies, it is assumed that a polar bear's fur functions in much the same way as a fiber optic cable. Light beams are conducted through the inside of each hair (or cable) by refraction. The polar bear uses this effect to produce heat by irradiation. This principle can be transferred to regulate and guide the light beams for controlled applications. The light-conducive fibers are structured, absorb the irradiation, and lead it to a layer, which thus serves energy generation. In this layer, the beams are turned into electrical energy. Depending on the position of the sun, the angle of the fibers can be changed by means of a 'pulling' tool. In contrast to polar bear hairs, the fibers are aerated and straight; therefore less heat develops just above the skin. Overheating could be avoided and the energy could be used selectively, which makes this principal very attractive for use in desert regions.

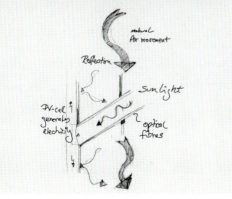
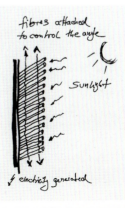

REVOLVING COLLECTOR
27-09-2006

IMAGINED BY Vincent van Sabben, Joep Hövels, Roel Philippa, Tess Zandbergen
KEYWORDS modular, phase-change material

A three-layer element consisting of PCM, insulation and a light-absorbing surface is arranged in a modular system that changes its direction according to the temperature. During the day, the PCM is oriented toward the sun in order to absorb energy. During the night, the module rotates 180° so that the PCM faces the interior space where it releases its energy to warm the room.

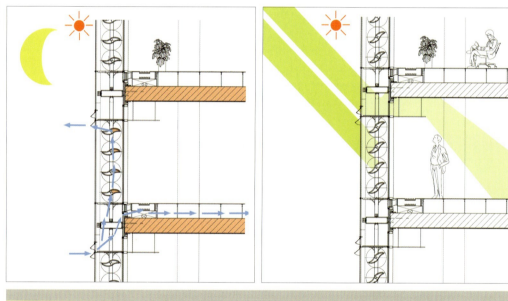

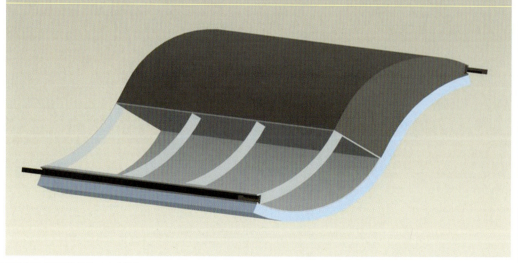

HAIR-PROTECTED FAÇADE
20-08-2007

IMAGINED BY Ari Bergsma, Marcel Bilow, Thiemo Ebert, Lidia Badarnah, Tillmann Klein, Ulrich Knaack, Holger Techen, Mathias Michel, Daan Rietbergen
KEYWORDS hair, ventilation, protection, natural

The hair protects the façade from rain and moisture, while air can still penetrate the façade through small openings that lead to the interior space.

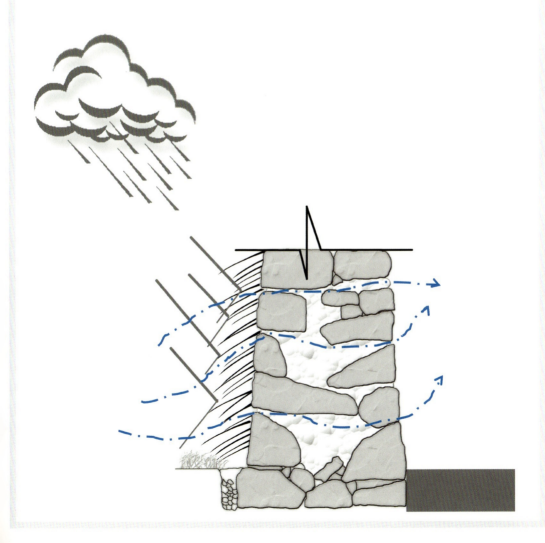

SHADING / VENTILATING FAÇADE
20-08-2007

IMAGINED BY Arie Bergsma, Marcel Bilow, Thiemo Ebbert, Tillmann Klein, Ulrich Knaack, Raymond Van Sabben, Lidia Badarnah, Daan Rietbergen, Holger Techen, Matthias Michel
KEYWORDS sensor, optic fibers, pores, network

The system has pores for ventilation and optic fibers for shading, which are connected to a network of sensors. They react to signals from these sensors and change their angle to let the light penetrate or block it. The pores allow the air to penetrate the façade and thus ventilate the interior space.

SKINNY FAÇADE
20-08-2007

IMAGINED BY Arie Bergsma, Marcel Bilow, Thiemo Ebbert, Tillmann Klein, Ulrich Knaack, Raymond Van Sabben, Lidia Badarnah, Daan Rietbergen, Holger Techen, Matthias Michel
KEYWORDS neuronal system, pores, hair, sensor

This façade has the ability to sense certain outside conditions through the hair that is attached to its exterior. The components of the hair are connected in a neuronal network, allowing them to transmit a signal to the pores instructing them to open or close. Thus, the pores serve the ventilation of the building as the hair reacts to environmental changes.

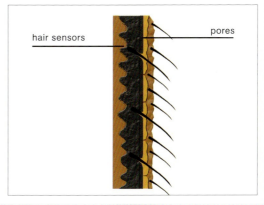

REFLECTION FAÇADE
06-07-2006

IMAGINED BY Linda Hildebrand
SUPPORTED BY Ulrich Knaack, Marcel Bilow
KEYWORDS constant reflection

Garment fabric developed by Sympatex features an aluminum-spattered surface that reflects 75% of the heat radiated from the body, thus preserving the body's temperature. The pores of all the layers are so small that they let vaporous sweat pass through but repel water. This principle can be reversed to reflect infrared light beams on the outside of a building, thus preventing the interior space from heating up. The carrier medium for the aluminum is a translucent membrane. It is waterproof and porous to air. Heat transfer caused by convection should be reduced by insulation. The middle layer serves as insulation and is translucent as well. The main purpose of the inside skin is to provide stability for the insulation, while allowing moisture in vapor form to escape through it. This principle could be used in latitudes near the equator, where temperatures are high.

Aluminum-spattered fabric by Schilgen, 0.2 mm aluminum allows reflection of IR radiation

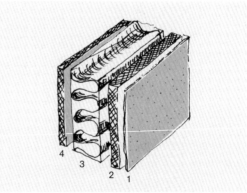

MAIN LAYERS : SPECIFICATIONS

- waterproof   1 is not waterproof, 2 keeps water out
- breatheable   all layers allow water vapor through
- radiation   1 reflects the majority of IR radiation, UV light is reflected. The goal is to have no additional light sources
- convection   3 repels hot air
- fire security with fire, all layers melt, do not ignite

SPONGE FAÇADE
06-07-2006

IMAGINED BY Linda Hildebrand
SUPPORTED BY Ulrich Knaack, Marcel Bilow
KEYWORDS chilling through evaporation

This façade principle is suited to hot regions. The innermost layer consists of a porous skin. A spongy fabric attached to this skin is moisturized with a liquid. The pores grow increasingly smaller from the inside to the outside, so that the evaporation happens near the inside surface. Here, the air cools down and passes through the thin layer to the interior space. The amount of liquid can be regulated according to the temperature. With current technology, water would be the obvious solution. However, a liquid that evaporates at lower temperatures would provide even better results because the air would cool down faster.

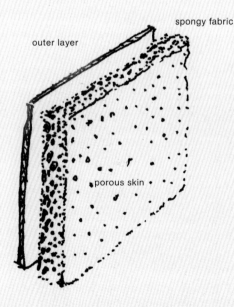
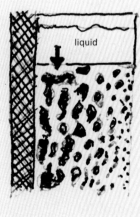

SPONGE RUBBER FAÇADE
20-07-2007

IMAGINED BY Thiemo Ebbert, Lourdes Lopez-Garrido
KEYWORDS free-form, ventilation, adaptable, low-cost, façade, 0-10 years

This project shows an easy way to solve the problem of cladding free-form structures. Why try to bend the filling material? Let's just bend the frames! Window frames and façade components are made from an elastic material, such as sponge rubber. Thus they can accommodate any direction and angle by compressing or stretching the frame material. The filling can be any of the commonly kind materials used for post-and-rail façades, such as glass or opaque panels.

FAÇADE HEATING / COOLING PANEL
15-08-2004

IMAGINED BY Marcel Bilow
KEYWORDS decentralized, heating /cooling, lightness, installations, concrete

To avoid the classical heating units in front of the glass surfaces, these unglazed units should be used as heating / cooling surfaces. The façade panels are made of fiber-reinforced concrete, embedded with textile. They are used for the load-bearing construction of the panels and can be inserted into the façade framework. The surface oriented towards the room is inlaid with areas of capillary tubes which cool the space in summer and heat it during winter. The use of fiber-reinforced concrete provides good heat conduction as well as stability.

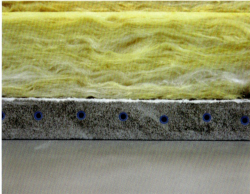

panel with standard radiator

oversized panel with additive radiator

heating elements integrated into the panel

ADAPTRONIC WINDOW HANDLE
29-08-2007

IMAGINED BY Marcel Bilow
ELABORATED BY Thomas Wiertel
KEYWORDS mono material, interactive, adaptable, technology transfer, aluminum

By using generative production procedures we might be able to realize complicated geometries and constructions that have not been feasible until the present. A window handle could be ergonomically integrated in a window aluminum profile. By adding adaptronic sensors in the same "printing" process, convenient control of the windows functions can be achieved. An RFID Chip Set could provide user-specific access levels. The integration of sensors in printed elements using rapid manufacturing technologies is still in its infancy, but when developed further, this technology will enable numerous newly emerging functionalities.

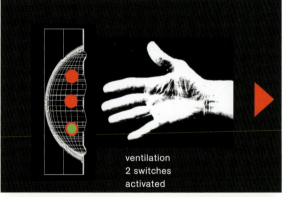

ventilation
2 switches
activated

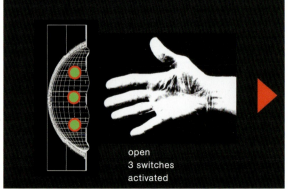

open
3 switches
activated

FUNARIA HYGROMETRICA - IRIS DIAPHRAGM
28-08-2007

IMAGINED BY Anika Börgers,
SUPPORTED BY Ulrich Knaack, Marcel Bilow
KEYWORDS bionic, mobile, adaptable, installations, unknown material

This is another idea based on the application of generative production procedures to realize complicated geometries and constructions. This idea for an operable lens is inspired by the geometric principle of the rotary moss (latin: funaria hygrometrica). Traditional camera apertures using iris diaphragms move on a two-dimensional plane and therefore require a certain amount of space around the perimeter. The aperture concept shown here uses less space because the aperture blades, when in the open position, are turned at a 90 degree angle. The size of an aperture element can vary from window size down to very small diameters with individual elements arranged in an array. The opening and closing action, and therefore regulation of light and solar radiation can be regulated by a switch. If the single elements are produced by means of rapid manufacturing, all functional geometries can be produced in a single process.

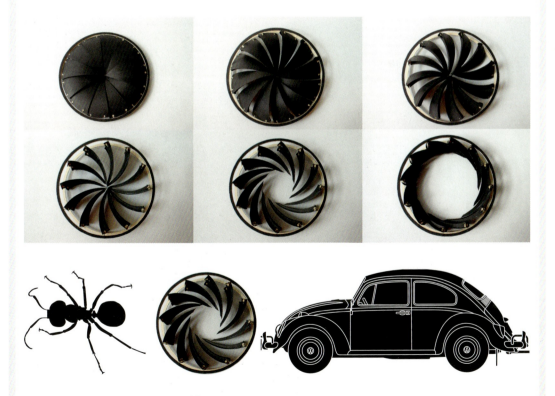

The system can be produced on different scales

FAÇADE SERVICE SLOT
23-10-2007

IMAGINED BY Ulrich Knaack
KEYWORDS integration, flexibility, fast-track assembly

This façade service slot can be used for the interaction of the façade with the mechanical services of a building. It can also fixate the façade. The element is mounted on the inside of the building, behind the façade. Fixing elements with a certain amount of tolerance make it easy to fit the façade service slot in the right position. In addition, this element could be used for ventilation.

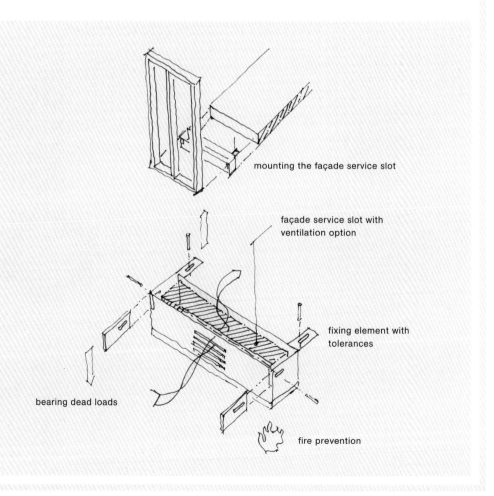

FLEXIBLE TEXTILE WINDOW / FISH-GILL FAÇADE
29-08-2007

IMAGINED BY Ulrich Knaack
ELABORATED BY Julia Makagon
SUPPORTED BY Marcel Bilow
KEYWORDS bionic, ventilation, transparency, façade, textile

The fish-gill principle could provide new solutions for the visibility and ventilation functions of a façade. A smart opening can be developed by using textile envelopes with an embedded steel rod or other flexible frame. With the help of smart materials, such as piezo-ceramic composites, the embedded rod could also move itself by using electricity impulses. The size of the openings could vary from window size down to a perforated area with minimal operable holes to create a more uniform look.

SELF-EXPANDING LINEAR JOINT
29-08-2007

IMAGINED BY M. Bilow
ELABORATED BY Nico Flötotto
KEYWORDS on-site, other functions, low-cost, system building, plastics

Sealing joints are usually made by injecting silicone or using pre-manufactured flexible profiles. An expanding foam profile that is compressed to minimum size under vacuum and covered with an airtight envelope will self-expand after assembly and inflation. These pressurized joints will also create load-bearing forces between the elements, holding them together tightly.

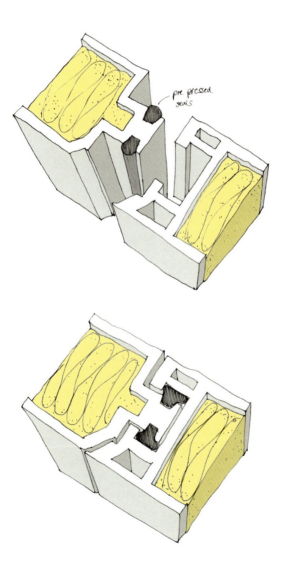

GLUED TEMPORARY CONSTRUCTION
08-02-2007

IMAGINED BY Kathrin Gröpper
KEYWORDS glued constructions, removable constructions, disassembly

Temporary constructions are often used for trade fair constructions or for art installations. The entire construction should be able to be built and removed within minutes. The structure should also be easily transportable. We could use an adhesive material that looses its adhesive properties when an electric current is applied. When the electric field is removed, the adhesive regains its agglomerating power. This process can be repeated as often as needed. Each wall element is equipped with electric cables and adhesive, and can be easily transported by the client. Electricity control is regulated via an external box to which the wall elements can be connected. If the bond is to be removed for dismantling, the box is connected to the element in question. The adhesive loosens on the cathode and remains on the element. The wall can be rebuilt without adding new glue by switching off the electric field.

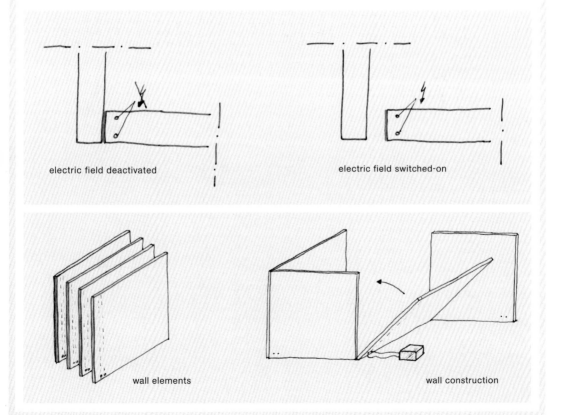

PLUG AND PLAY
27-09-2006

IMAGINED BY Thiemo Ebbert
KEYWORDS prefabrication, modular, system, façade, refurbishment

Why don't we change the appearance of a building like we change our clothing to suit fashion, climate and technical development? Buildings could be constructed in such a way that the envelope and installations can be changed or upgraded most easily. When fashion changes or demands on energy-savings rise, it is easy to replace elements of the building skin. A building can initially be enveloped for little money; and a few years later, when business is running well, you can buy more expensive, representative, highly efficient modules. Façade constructions are attached to standard fittings ("Isofix" connection). Installations are fully compatible and supplied with plug-and-play connections for electricity, IT, heating, water, etc. The building cradle brings the modules in place.
This requires sustainable and lightweight envelope constructions that are produced ecologically. They can be fully reused and recycled. We will see a flourishing market with second-hand façades on eBay. Façades that might be out of fashion in the Netherlands are sold in Germany, for example, or the other way around.

ENERGY STORING BRICK
07-11-2007

IMAGINED BY Marcel Bilow, Jens Böke, Ulrich Knaack
KEYWORDS energy storage, thermal mass

The basis of this idea was the concept of storing thermal energy in façades or collecting the energy by means of the façade. The façade itself is developed out of lightweight materials with an integrated storage tank for water. This water tank can be filled after positioning the unit as a "façade brick", so that the construction, in terms of building physics, then becomes a "heavy construction". Solar energy is collected on the outside of the façade and stored in the water tank until it is needed to warm the interior space. Alternatively, the same system can be used for cooling.

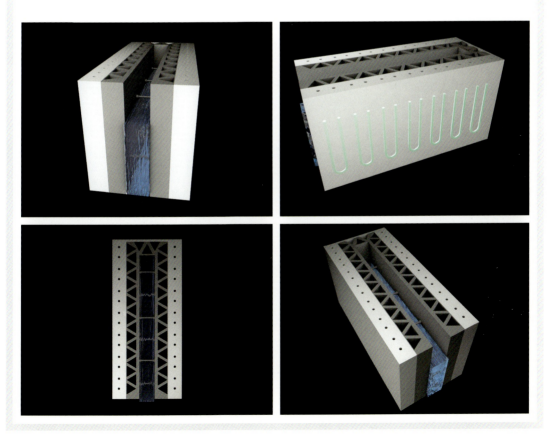

BOTTLE CASE FAÇADE
11-06-07

IMAGINED BY Ulrich Knaack
KEYWORDS low-cost, modular, system

Water-bottle carrier cases, foil, and water can offer a low-cost yet efficient façade.
A wall built of piled-up cases, enveloped by a foil, is filled with water. Ropes stabilize the cases; a frame attaches the wall to ceiling and floor. Because the water is filled into small chambers, the massive filling insulates with the occurrence of hardly any convection.

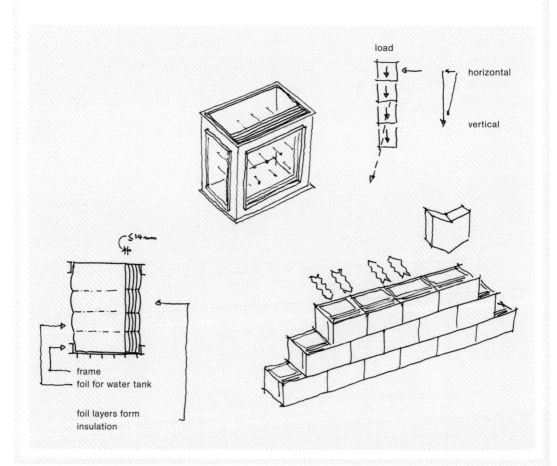

(RE)FOLDABLES
03-07-2007

IMAGINED BY Tillmann Klein, Arie Bergsma, Tina Van Houten
KEYWORDS (re)foldables, temporary structure, lightweight, composites

One of the easiest ways to create a strong structure out of plane elements is to fold them. Origami, the ancient Japanese art of paper folding, uses this principle and it inspired the idea to develop (re)foldable structures that could be useful as temporary buildings such as exhibition spaces, musical stages, shelters, etc. Take the case where an exhibition is in Rotterdam one month and in Amsterdam the next, for example. The (re)foldable building is the solution. A (re)foldable building has many advantages compared to the traditional building methods. The structure can be made of very light material, consists of fewer elements, is easy to transport and quickly assembled.

(Re)foldable hospital

(Re)foldable festival tent

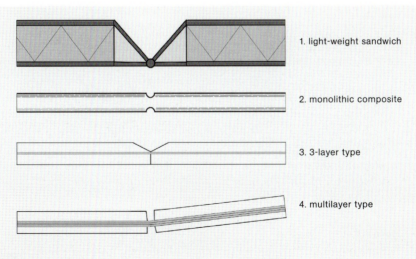

Possible folding systems

1. light-weight sandwich
2. monolithic composite
3. 3-layer type
4. multilayer type

(RE)FOLDABLE PAVILION
03-07-2007

IMAGINED BY Tillmann Klein, Arie Bergsma, Tina Van Houten
KEYWORDS (re)foldables, temporary structure, lightweight, composites

Within the scope of developing (re)foldable structures, a lightweight pavilion (bicycle repair shop) was planned for the campus of Delft University of Technology. This pavilion shows the use of composites in architecture. The design of this temporary pavilion uses lightweight sandwich panels with a thermally insulated core and fiber-reinforced surfaces. The hinges consist of rubber strips. Zips could be used to connect the individual structural parts of the (re)foldable structure and to make the structure watertight.
The development of this pavilion was part of the workshop entitled Vision of Lightness, held at the TU Delft in December 2007. During this workshop, groups of students and researchers worked together in teams with representatives of the composite industry to develop several lightweight composite pavilions.

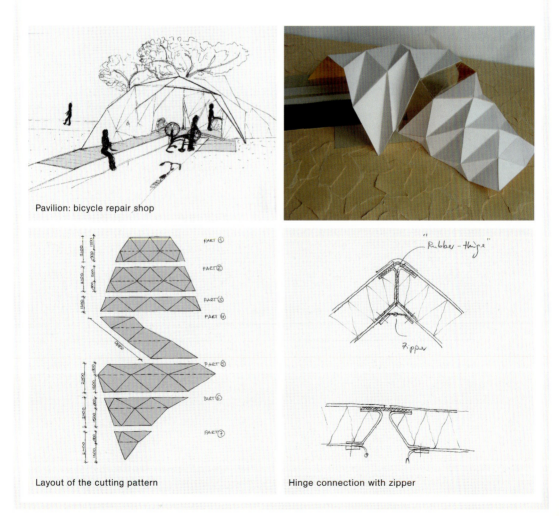

Pavilion: bicycle repair shop

Layout of the cutting pattern

Hinge connection with zipper

(RE)FOLDABLE EXHIBITION WALL
03-07-2007

IMAGINED BY Tillmann Klein, Arie Bergsma, Tina Van Houten
KEYWORDS (re)foldables, temporary structure, lightweight, composites

Another project within the scope of developing (re)foldable structures was a design for a lightweight exhibition wall for the chair of Design of Constructions, which could be easily transported and dismantled. Posters could be attached to the folded walls for presentation purposes. The (re)foldable wall system consists of stiff panels made of sandwich constructions or PC plates. The hinges are made of flexible rubber or textile connections. The proposed exhibition wall consists of two large elements that can be interconnected. Of course, additional elements can easily be fitted on, allowing for more spatial configurations.

Exhibition wall

INTERWOVEN TEXTILE FAÇADE
29-08-2007

IMAGINED BY Nely Kornelsen
SUPPORTED BY Ulrich Knaack, Marcel Bilow
KEYWORDS layered construction, insulation, lightness, façade, textile

According to the latest three dimensional weaving and stitching technologies, an envelope made out of different functional properties could be made out of textiles. The idea shown here combines two layers of woven textiles that are combined by a sealing layer. Different functions related to the materials used could enhance the properties of the overall building envelope.
- Capillary heating pipes – cooling and heating.
- PCM – heat storage.

The design could vary depending on the specific technology used.

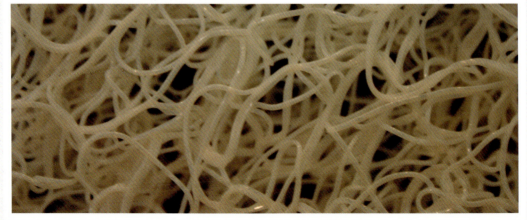

FIBER-CONCRETE FAÇADE POSTS
10-11-2007

IMAGINED BY Ulrich Knaack, Marcel Bilow
KEYWORDS system, load bearing, solid, façade, concrete

The typical materials currently used for post and beam façades are aluminum, steel and wood. Only aluminum sections contain all the necessary parts for joining and fixing in one extruded profile. Using wood or steel usually requires an aluminum profile that is attached to the load bearing beams to meet the fixing and sealing requirements. Looking more closely at these elements, other materials could perhaps provide a broader range of possibilities. In this concept, fiber-reinforced concrete profiles, formed into their final shape by pultrusion, could also fulfill load-bearing requirements.

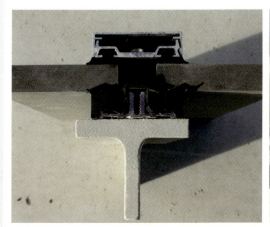
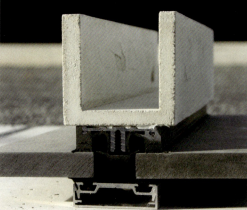
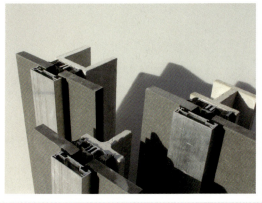
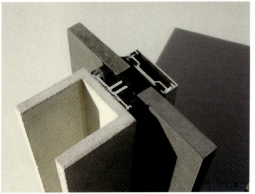

SNAKESKIN
06-07-2006

IMAGINED BY Linda Hildebrand
SUPPORTED BY Ulrich Knaack, Marcel Bilow
KEYWORDS elastic skin

The skin of a snake has qualities that can be transferred to building technology in areas jeopardized by earthquakes. The façade developed according to this concept uses waxy scales that, when slack, protect against solar irradiation and humidity. The scales are interwoven with their medium so that they cannot detach. If the walls stretch during an earthquake, the arrangement is less dense but the medium layer can withstand enormous elongation. The core piece of this façade principle is the insulation, which is connected to the elastic skin that covers it on both sides at very few points only. If the ceilings, to which the façade is attached, move and stretch, and the distance between one story and the next changes, the two elastic walls stretch along with the insulation within. An earthquake-safe construction must comprise a façade that endures shock.

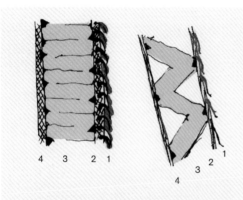

1 scales layer
2 sustaining layer
3 heat insulation
4 inner skin

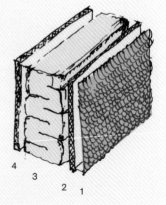

Insulation is only attached at a few points. In a case of emergency the insulation transforms

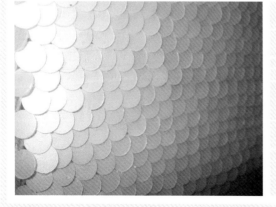

MAIN LAYERS : SPECIFICATIONS

- waterproof   1 is not waterproof, 2 keeps water out

- breatheable   all layers transmit evaporated water

- radiation   1 if necessary has different degrees of reflection

- convection   3 blocks hot air from penetration

- fire security   in cases of fire, all layers melt and do not spread the fire

3-D MULTIPLEX
3-D CONCRETE STRUCTURE
SUPER EXCLUSIVE SANDWICHES
GRADED WALL
POPCORN FAÇADE
FIBER CONCRETE FAÇADE
FEM-DRIVEN STRUCTURES
EXTRUSION MOLD
FOLDING A CONSTRUCTION
INTEGRATED SANDWICH CONSTRUCTION / JACKBOX
MOLDING FOAM FOR FREELY CURVED PANELS
FREELY CURVED METAL PU-PANELS
GLASS LEGO BRICKS
MEDIUM-INSERTED GLASS
GLASS SANDWICH
FOLDED GLASS
WELDED GLASS
IN-SITU GLASS / ORTGLAS
ZIPPER SANDWICH

2.3. MATERIALS

Plastics, metal foam, composites, coating and self-organization are only some of the keywords to describe the impact of materials on the future of façade. Developed for specific applications such as military use or for the aeronautic industry, the materials are thoroughly tested and, if successfully applied, transferred to architecture.
Plastics are an important topic these days as they are comparably easy to produce in different forms such as films or fibers. The name is derived from plasticity, the ability to deform – the core quality of this material. Their great potential lies in the diverse application possibilities. The ability to be combined with other materials is another important advantage of plastics. The quality and characteristics of these composites can be specified according to specific requirements. The advantageous properties of individual materials are combined to generate a product with certain improved qualities. For example, a strong construction made with fiber-reinforced concrete is much lighter than one made with solid concrete. In addition to improved effectiveness, the number of possible shapes also rises dramatically.
A new generation of materials comprises 'self-organizing materials'. The focus in current research lies on developing intelligent devices. A construction that reacts to an increasing force by supporting the structure itself or configures that change according to user requirements are both upcoming ideas. And new production technologies have been and are being developed: CAD (computer-aided design) was one of the major influences on architecture during the last decade. It enabled more complex, more efficient and more diverse structures and designs. This tool enabled planners to control huge systems. The limitations of CAD become obvious during the realization phase. Existing production techniques cannot always implement what the computer is able to generate. CAM provides a solution to bridges this gap: Computer Aided Manufacturing designates the interface between the PC modelled product and the production technique. The digitalization of the product chain gives a wide populacee access to individual products. Rapid prototyping defines the process in which 3-D devices are shaped out of a formless media. What hitherto was reserved for the car industry, for machines or the airplane industry is now incorporated into architecture. These innovative materials and procedure impact the perception of the façade in an essential way. The new options will have to be implemented into the façade – a new technology, but certainly not the last.

3-D MULTIPLEX
02-07-2006

IMAGINED BY Ulrich Knaack
KEYWORDS layered construction, structure, load-bearing, wood

The load-bearing capacity of wood works in only one direction. Multiplex by Kerto uses a combination of several layers of wood, arranged in different orientation, to provide the possibility of using wood as a monolithic material with 2-directional load-bearing capability. The idea of this 3-D Multiplex material was to create a wood material that can be used for all three dimensions of load-bearing structures. Combining wood elements in all three directions also results in a reduction of the dead load by 1/4.

Imagine 01 MATERIALS

3-D CONCRETE STRUCTURE
15-05-2006

IMAGINED BY Ulrich Knaack, Marcel Bilow
KEYWORDS composite, energy generating, load-bearing, free-form, organic, textile, 3-D fabrics, concrete

The idea involves the possibilities of 3-dimensional woven structures stabilized by concrete. This concepts includes possible integration of components for insulation, energy collection (water pipes etc) and transparency.

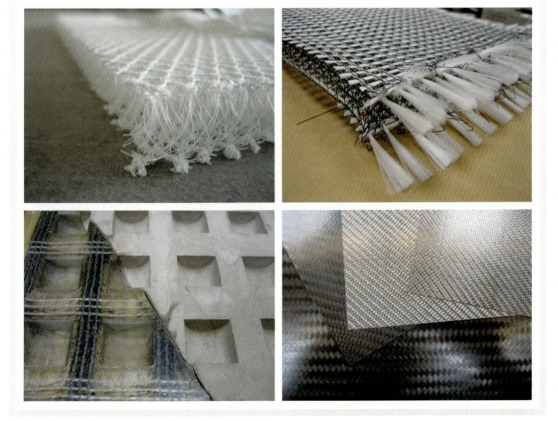

SUPER EXCLUSIVE SANDWICHES
10-05-2006

IMAGINED BY Ulrich Knaack, Daan Rietbergen
KEYWORDS layered constructions, composite, load-bearing, lightness, façade, roof, composite

Sandwiches are made of a combination of different materials. For claddings, many combinations are imaginable in order to create lighter, cheaper or stronger panels, and probably a combination of these characteristics. This concept has been developed to produce super-sized panels with exclusive materials such as mahogany wood or marble – materials usually unmanageable and unaffordable.

GRADED WALL
31-03-2007

IMAGINED BY Thomas Auer, Marcel Bilow, Mathias Rudolph
KEYWORDS composite, envelope, vision, load-bearing, composite, lightness

Functionally graded materials are materials which exhibit a gradient (continuous or stepped) in composition, porosity, grain size, level of magnetization, level of polarization etc. Therefore their properties depend on the position within the material. The gradient can be one-dimensional or multidimensional. The graded wall is a sandwich construction which combines several functional areas. The functions change using the gradient principle; e.g. all the changes from a load-bearing function to an energy-gaining zone. Different functions are possible by arranging separate functions side by side. The wall is highly flexible in terms of separating its functions. Each requirement can be realized in different size and position. Appearance and functionality go hand in hand; the wall is structure, façade, sun-shading, insulation, energy generator…. Smart sun-shading can be realized by inserting manipulators into the honeycomb gaps.

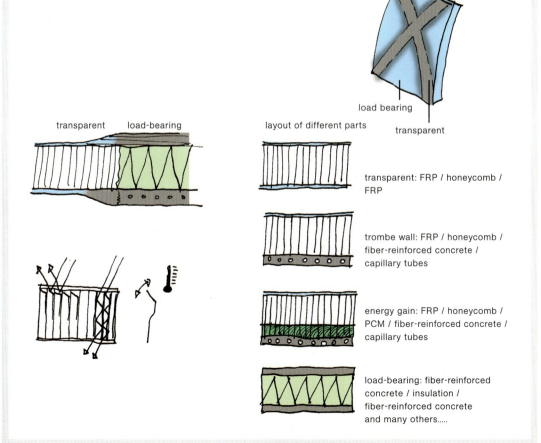

POPCORN FAÇADE
11-06-07

IMAGINED BY Arie Bergsma, Marcel Bilow, Thiemo Ebbert, Tillmann Klein, Ulrich Knaack, Raymond Van Sabben, Lidia Badarnah, Daan Rietbergen, Volker Techen, Matthias Michel
KEYWORDS shapeable insulation, deflated, vision, onsite, free-form onsite, free-form, insulation

Just like popcorn expanding its volume when heated, insulation could behave in a similar way by developing its full volume at the location where it is to be installed. Surrounded by foil, the material in the space between functions as a spacer. Any desirable form is thinkable, as the panel remains its form when all air is sucked out. Another advantage of this principle is the low transport cost.

FIBER CONCRETE FAÇADE
28-06-2006

IMAGINED BY Ulrich Knaack, Marcel Bilow
KEYWORDS layered construction, composite, load-bearing, low-cost, structure, façade concrete, textiles

Within the course of glass constructions, a modular façade made of fiber-reinforced concrete with an integrated building-services element was developed. Up to the present, the main materials employed were the traditional materials used in extensive curtain walls, such as aluminum, steel, wood and glass. The development of fiber-reinforced concrete makes it possible to produce slim profiles and frames that can almost achieve the dimensions of those manufactured in aluminum or steel. The concept of a modular façade made of fiber-reinforced concrete shows the future field of application of this material as an extension of existing scopes for design. Fiber-reinforced concrete has been commonly used for façade constructions, namely the panels for curtain walls; however, its utilization for the load-bearing elements of façades is new. With a thickness of only 60mm, the mock-up model still shows a large potential for further development. The supporting pillars are filled with rigid foam and have an average thickness of 10mm.

This project was supported by the companies: Metallbau Holz / Leopoldshöhe (elements of the façade and glass), Fa. Durapact / Haan (fiber-reinforced concrete), Fa. Krülland / Kaarst (shading device).

FEM-DRIVEN STRUCTURES
29-08-2007

IMAGINED BY Ulrich Knaack, Marcel Bilow
ELABORATED BY Heiko Oexle
KEYWORDS self-organizing, load-bearing, strength, structure, unknown material

This principle is based on the fact that generative production procedures can now generate complicated geometries and previously insoluble constructions.
According to the principles of bionic bone structures, material is only placed where the forces connect to the structure. Thus, you can detect the regions where the forces interact by applying a finite element analysis (FEM), lightweight structures can easily be designed. Material on zero lines/forces can be minimized or completely eliminated. Using rapid manufacturing technologies, load-bearing structures seem possible with materials such as steel or aluminum, to create effective and lightweight façade structures.

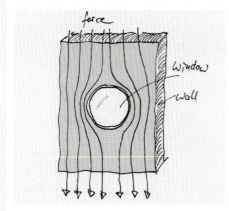
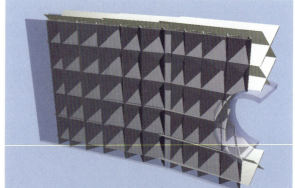
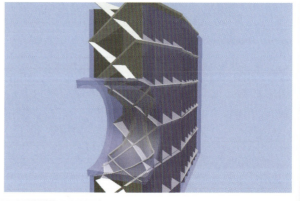

EXTRUSION MOLD
15-05-2006

IMAGINED BY Tillmann Klein
KEYWORDS free form, economic, adaptable, tool, 0-10 years, unknown material

The aim is to create a tool that continuously produces free-form elements that can be assembled into a bigger structure. The extrusion mold can be adjusted in two dimensions. The third dimension is introduced by the flow of the material itself. Temperatures, pressure, speed of the process are important factors. Flexible core-materials can be introduced. Reinforcement of the outer material can be done with fibers. The cooled material is to be cut into certain sizes. Different edge types can be produced with complex cutting machines. If a load-bearing construction is necessary, the parts will only need to be formed in two dimensions as result of the rectangular projection of the elements.

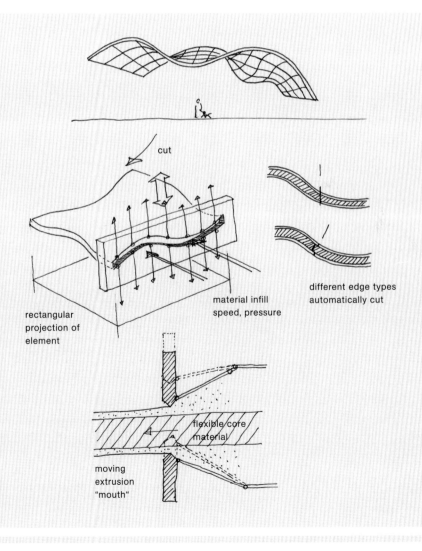

FOLDING A CONSTRUCTION
10-05-2006

IMAGINED BY Ulrich Knaack, Marcel Bilow, Daan Rietbergen
KEYWORDS layered construction, composite, load-bearing, strength, structure, composite

This idea uses standard sandwich panels to create furniture, for example. By milling out splices, a panel can be folded into any application. Many shapes are possible; a study needs to be done in folding techniques.

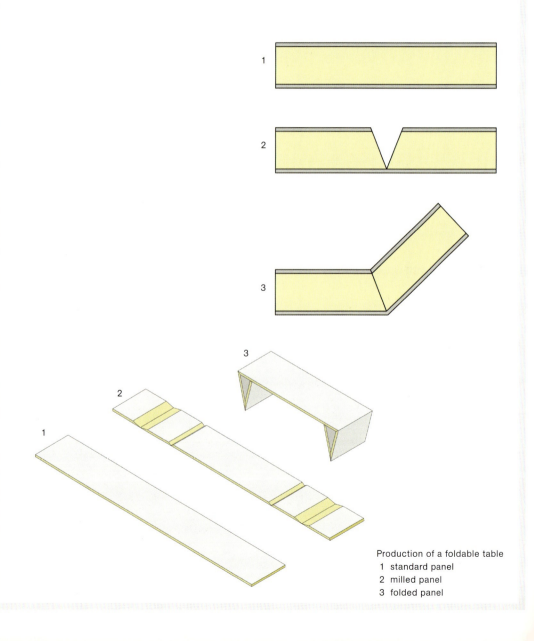

Production of a foldable table
1 standard panel
2 milled panel
3 folded panel

INTEGRATED SANDWICH CONSTRUCTION / JACKBOX
01-05-2007

IMAGINED BY Ulrich Knaack, Marcel Bilow, Tillman Klein
KEYWORDS composite, load-bearing, lightness, system building, composite

The idea of the JACKBOX project is based on a sensible combination of technical possibilities and intelligent materials in order to produce multifunctional system components. The sandwich panels are made by means of vacuum processing, and consist of the following elements: external GRP skin as weatherproof coating, sandwich core made of PU foam for heat insulation, and an inside layer of fiber-reinforced concrete with integrated capillary pipe mats.
The fiber-reinforced concrete layer provides cooling/heating through the capillary pipes, as well as additional temperature control due to its thermal mass, and efficient radiation heating. The parts of the building conceived as single modules were produced as one large GRP sandwich with a fiberglass-reinforced plastic skin and hard foam core, and then cut to size. The panels can be folded by incisions in the roof area. After the elements are fixed in the desired form, the inside surface of textile-reinforced concrete with inlaid capillary pipes was sprayed.

This project was supported by the following companies: Fa. Dorapact / Haan, Fa. Arthermo / Rad Oezn Hausen, Fa. Pecocar / Emschedz, Fa. Essmaxim/Bad Salz Uflem, Fa. Doorliuz / Leopolds Efgyz

Imagine 01 MATERIALS

MOLDING FOAM FOR FREELY CURVED PANELS
10-05-2006

IMAGINED BY Ulrich Knaack, Daan Rietbergen
KEYWORDS layered constructions, composite, load-bearing, lightness, façade, roof, composite

By using a two-sided adjustable mould, a freely curved volume can be formed with foam. To keep the foam in place, a temporary plastic bag can be used. After the foam has stiffened, the sides are cut off by laser and the shape is finished with fibers and epoxies.

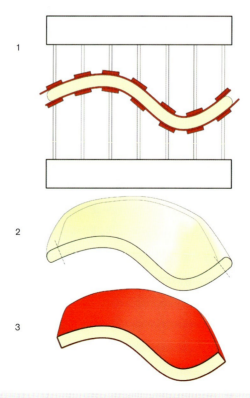

FREELY CURVED METAL PU-PANELS
10-05-2006

IMAGINED BY Ulrich Knaack, Daan Rietbergen
KEYWORDS layered constructions, free-form, composite, load-bearing, lightness, façade, roof, composite

This concept was developed to produce freely curved sandwich panels with a PU-core and an aluminum surface. The method is described in the following pictures. The panels can be of varying thickness, giving extra stiffness to certain parts of the panel. Extra stiffness is also possible by using polyurethane of varying density.

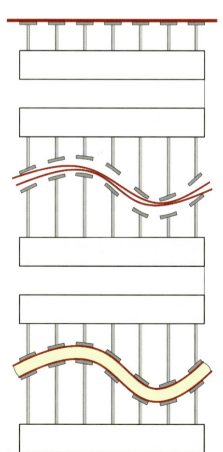

Two sheets (e.g. aluminum) are positioned between two adjustable moulds

The moulds take their position, the sheets are pressed into form

By injecting the polyurethane, the sheets are given their final shape

Next step would be the detailing of the panel

GLASS LEGO BRICKS
23-10-2007

IMAGINED BY Ulrich Knaack
KEYWORDS glass construction, load-bearing, glass

With these glass Lego bricks you can build glass walls quickly and without any glue or cement. Each glass Lego brick is built the same way; therefore they can all be fitted to one another. To fixate them, a piece of rubber is inserted between two bricks. The wall can even be built in a circle of at least 51°.

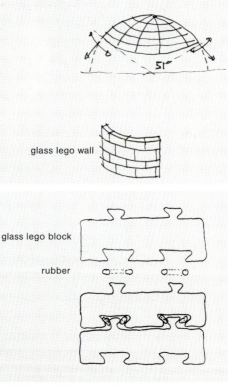

glass lego wall

glass lego block

rubber

MEDIUM-INSERTED GLASS
15-06-2006

IMAGINED BY Ulrich Knaack, Marcel Bilow
PICTURES BY Michael Schmitz
KEYWORDS layered construction, energy generating, sun-shading, transparency, liquid, façade, building physics, glass, 10-20 years

In the future, glass welding or gluing will be just as possible as molding it into any desired shape. The idea is to create glass panels out of two base panes that are glued or welded together – remaining highly transparent – to create a waterproof channel system within the resulting chamber. If the chamber is filled with transparent or colored media such as water or oil, we can achieve a wide range of solutions serving various functionalities.
The panels could be used as:
- Sun-shading components
- Energy-generating collectors
- Shutters or blinds

The grid of the medium channels could be adjusted according to the desired functions.

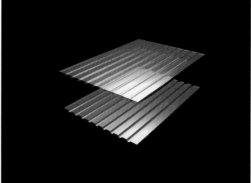
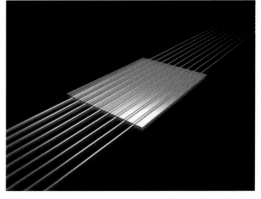

GLASS SANDWICH
15-06-2006

IMAGINED BY Ulrich Knaack, Marcel Bilow
PICTURES BY Michael Schmitz
KEYWORDS layered construction, transparency, roof, lighting, building physics, glass, 10-20 years

In the future, glass welding or gluing will be just as possible as molding it into any desired shape. The idea is to create glass panels from two panes glued or welded together, while remaining highly transparent, with glass spacers to create a load-bearing sandwich that can be used for roofs or façades. To support the internal forces, the spacers are arranged at closer intervals on the corners of the panels. Using these elements as highly transparent roof sections, it is posssible to build a museum with a natural incidenccee of light without windows or façades. So new spaces and sites in the city will be possible due to light from above.

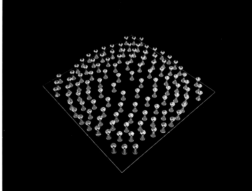
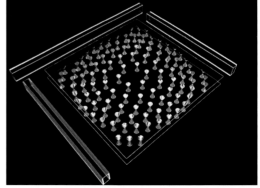

FOLDED GLASS
16-06-2006

IMAGINED BY Ulrich Knaack, Marcel Bilow
PICTURES BY Torben Inderhees
KEYWORDS mono material, free form, load-bearing, transparency, solid, façade, roof, structure, 10-20 years, glass

In the future, glass could be formed into shapes similar to steel or other metals today. A tool by means of which a glass pane can be heated in specific places and then bent could provide a folded glass construction. Folded glass elements could be compiled to create a transparent structure.

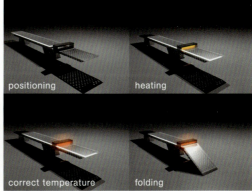

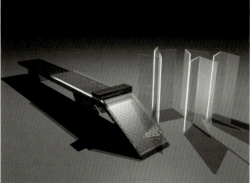

WELDED GLASS
16-06-2006

IMAGINED BY Ulrich Knaack, Marcel Bilow
PICTURES BY Torben Inderhees
KEYWORDS mono material, free-form, load-bearing, transparency, solid, façade, roof, structure, 10-20 years, glass

Welding glass might be possible in the future. If so, it will be possible to create free-form, highly transparent, load-bearing structures shaped like the roof of the trade center in Milan, but without the steel. Pieces of molded curved glass trimmed in exact shapes are welded together on the site. Only a supporting structure that holds the panes in position during the welding is necessary. After welding the glass, diamond grinding tools smooth the welding seams into a highly transparent, monolithic glass envelope.

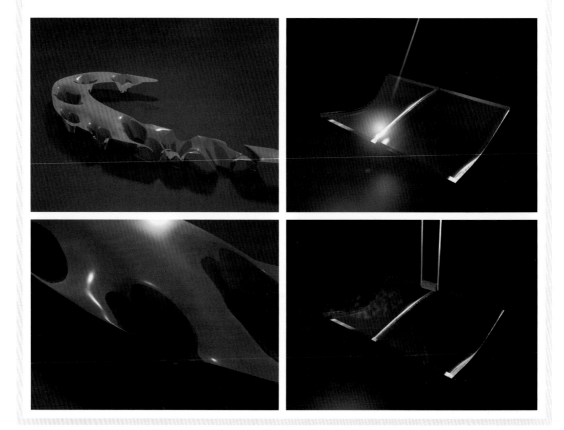

IN-SITU GLASS / ORTGLAS
16-06-2006

IMAGINED BY Torben Inderhees
SUPPORTED BY Ulrich Knaack, Marcel Bilow
KEYWORDS mono material, free form, load-bearing, transparency, solid, façade, roof, structure, 10-20 years, glass

In-situ glass might be possible in the future. Molding glass in-situ like concrete is an idea to create free form or rectangular shapes out of monolithic glass. The mold has to resist the high temperature of the liquid glass. Reinforcement of the "site glass" is possible with woven or knitted glass fiber textiles, thus creating glass textiles that are highly transparent when the liquid glass is inserted into the mold. Various surface types can be achieved by using different molding surfaces.

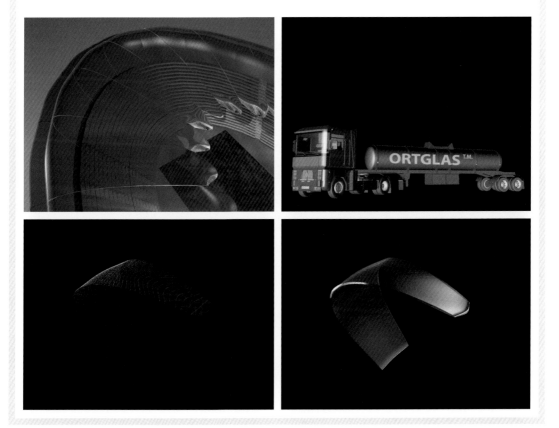

ZIPPER SANDWICH
10-05-2006

IMAGINED BY Ulrich Knaack, Daan Rietbergen
KEYWORDS layered constructions, free-form, composite, load bearing, lightness, façade, roof, composite

Freely (single) curved panels can be produced by using the principle of the castellated beam. These panels could be used for cladding blob buildings or for providing improved structural capability.

By injecting polyurethane, the system will expand, fold and clamp

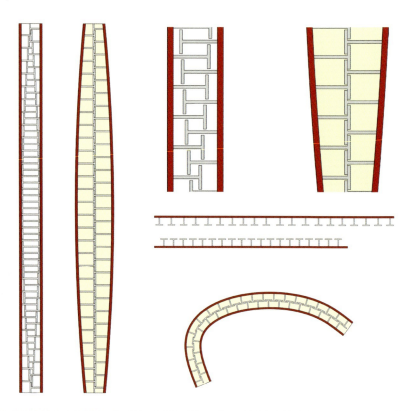

Imagine 01 FAÇADES

VIRTUAL FAÇADE
DARK SKIN
TEMPORARY DRESS
EYE EFFECT
GOOSE BUMPS
AIRPLANE SKIN
WIND-STOP COVER
CHAMELEON
HUMAN SKIN
MOIRÉ FAÇADE
ELECTROSTATIC DUST FAÇADE
HOW ARE YOU TODAY?
BIO HEAT

2.4. ADAPTABLE

As a result of changing user demands and developing production techniques, the requirements of façades are now having to be adapted. Whereas this outer skin of a building has hitherto been regarded as a protective system with a passive character, its pretensions are now being modified. The modern façade could be able to sense changes in the environment and react to them, as well as respond to changing user requirements. Intelligent envelopes should follow the development of demands such as temperature requirements and light regulation and air-conditioning.

Instead of simply heating in winter and cooling in summer, an adaptable façade will react to the environment by changing its qualities to focus on the situation in a holistic way. Industry and nature are ahead of façade technology with existing solutions; thus, these need to be imported into our discipline. They give impulses to create new ideas for reactive façade systems. The façade is losing its mono-functionality as an envelope and is becoming an integrative system which reacts to changes in climate and user requirements.

VIRTUAL FAÇADE
23-10-2007

IMAGINED BY Ulrich Knaack
KEYWORDS virtual, glass, transparency

The idea behind this façade is being able to choose your personal façade. The user can choose his or her favorite interior surface. The appearance can reflect the weather, a location or an emotion. On the outside of the building, the chosen image appears on an LED screen covering the entire façade. The appearance can be changed at certain time intervals, by the user or centrally controlled by the owner.

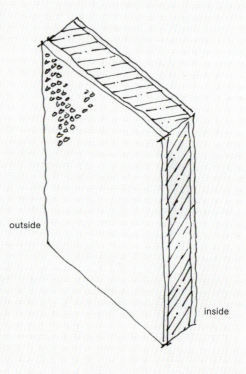

DARK SKIN
11-05-2006

IMAGINED BY Linda Hildebrand
SUPPORTED BY Ulrich Knaack, Marcel Bilow
KEYWORDS heat control by organizing pigments

Darker skin contains more pigments than light skin. This difference is important for processing vitamins. Light-skinned people need more sunlight to generate vitamins. In the regions closer to the equator, where the people are more severely exposed to the sun, a comprehensive protection against the ultraviolet rays is needed. A façade that reacts to solar irradiation could contribute to reducing the cooling load inside a building. Pigments could be arranged in specific structures by sensor technology. In cases of intense radiation the pigments are spread evenly, whereas they are arranged in clusters when there is less solar irradiation. The pictured pigments are able to store light and emit it after the light has gone.

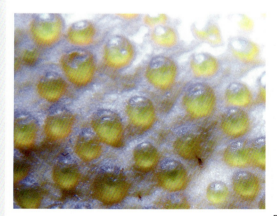
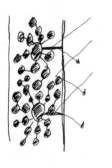

Pigment clusters spread out under sunlight to minimize solar irradiation

TEMPORARY DRESS
11-05-2006

IMAGINED BY Linda Hildebrand
SUPPORTED BY Ulrich Knaack, Marcel Bilow
KEYWORDS wind stop, isolating layer

A winter jacket uses three layers to protect against wind and cold. The outside layer serves as wind and rain protection. The middle layer is filled with a less dense material, which is voluminous and provides a spacer between the inside and outside layer. The inside layer is porous and fixed to the outside layer. It often consists of cotton, allows air to penetrate, and is thicker than the outside layer but not waterproof. We could construct a wall system in which the insulation layer is only inserted during cold periods and is removed in summer. This would be attractive for houses whose insulation does not meet modern standards.

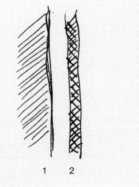

1 body
2 sweatshirt
3 lining
4 insulation-air mixture
5 windproof layer

EYE EFFECT
10-05-2006

IMAGINED BY Linda Hildebrand
SUPPORTED BY Ulrich Knaack, Marcel Bilow
KEYWORDS reaction to light

The human eye reacts to different lighting conditions. The pupil is minimized or enlarged by the movement of the muscles in order to control the incoming light. When the pupil closes, the whole spectrum of light is detained. A façade equipped with a closing mechanism could regulate the lighting conditions. If strong solar irradiation occurs, the façade should close. If the sky is cloudy, the opening should become larger so that more light reaches the inside of the building.

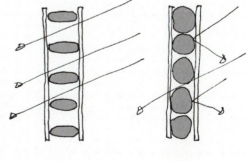

When there are clouds more beams can pass through

Intense radiation is kept out with an insulating layer

GOOSE BUMPS
22-05-2006

IMAGINED BY Linda Hildebrand
SUPPORTED BY Ulrich Knaack, Marcel Bilow
KEYWORDS insulation when necessary

If a human being feels cold, the body hair stands up. The skin surface changes and reminds us of a plucked goose, the term's eponym. This mechanism serves to increase the layer between the cold environment and the skin. The hair on our skin prevents the body heat from disappearing. This additional layer is used only when required. A façade with this adaptability could be an energy saving solution.

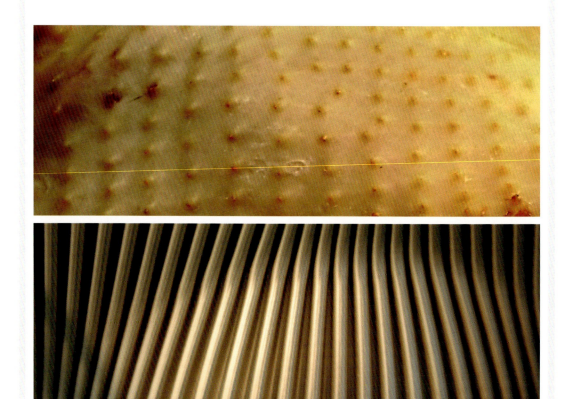

AIRPLANE SKIN
23-05-2006

IMAGINED BY Linda Hildebrand
SUPPORTED BY Ulrich Knaack, Marcel Bilow
KEYWORDS minimum friction

The outer shell of an airplane is formed to generate the least air resistance. The transfer of this technology to skyscrapers would allow a thinner construction due to the reduced wind load. The outer shell of Airbus A380 is made of "Glare", glass-fiber-reinforced aluminum. It consists of several 0.3 mm thick aluminum sheets, glue foils, and fiber-glass foils. Its most important advantages are the light weight and its surface. This concept is taken from nature. Shark skin has extremely little flow resistance. With its regular flute structure and the rough shark skin, great distances can be realized with comparably little energy.

WIND-STOP COVER
06-07-2006

IMAGINED BY Linda Hildebrand
SUPPORTED BY Ulrich Knaack, Marcel Bilow
KEYWORDS temporary coat

Airflow is an important factor for heat generation. In summer, a cool breeze refreshes the body and in winter it takes the warm air away and promotes cooling. The wind-stopper is a skin to be used only in winter. It is attached to the existing façade, and is very attractive for glassy skyscrapers because a high amount of warmth dissipates with the wind. The greater the distance to the ground, the stronger the wind. Insulation glass attempts to prevent this heat loss. The wind-stopper disturbs the cooling process and contributes to efficient energy use. To gain maximum benefit of this effect, only a temporary use is advisable.

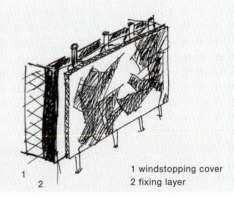

1 windstopping cover
2 fixing layer

MAIN LAYERS : SPECIFICATIONS	
• waterproof	1 is waterproof
• breatheable	1 lets only evaporated water penetrate
• radiation	1 reflects UV radiation, IR and visual light pass through
• convection	1 does not keep out convection
• fire security	1 and 2 evaporate or melt in fire

CHAMELEON
13-05-2006

IMAGINED BY Linda Hildebrand
SUPPORTED BY Ulrich Knaack, Marcel Bilow
KEYWORDS temperature regulation by light

The chameleon is able to adapt its appearance to the color of its surroundings, so that it is invisible for an enemy but highly visible for a potential mate. The lighting conditions and temperature determine this process. If the temperature of the animal's skin is low, it becomes darker, so that the skin absorbs the light more rather than reflecting it. The principle can be transferred to a façade: the proportion between reflection and absorption affects the temperature. The analogy would be a façade whose color is determined by the interior temperature.

HUMAN SKIN
13-05-2006

IMAGINED BY Linda Hildebrand
SUPPORTED BY Ulrich Knaack, Marcel Bilow
KEYWORDS breathing house, temperature regulation by moisture contribution

The human skin regulates its temperature with the help of sweat, which enables it to react to external temperature changes. The outside skin layer is relatively thin and serves as a protection from injuries to the layer beneath. Its healing process is relatively rapid. An underlying fat layer protects the interior organs against variations in temperature and mechanical injuries. If the body is severely exposed to the sun, the skin is affected first. For protection against temperature rise and burning, the skin releases sweat and, in combination with moving air, cools down. Furthermore, the sunbeams volatilize the moisture before they affect the skin. A façade based on this principle could be made up of four layers, with the outside layer releasing moisture at high temperatures to provide a cooling effect.

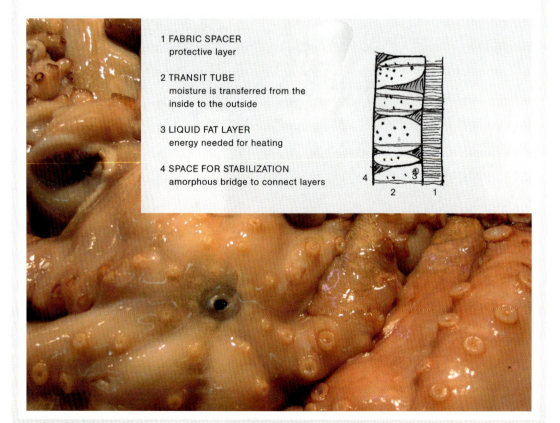

1 FABRIC SPACER
protective layer

2 TRANSIT TUBE
moisture is transferred from the inside to the outside

3 LIQUID FAT LAYER
energy needed for heating

4 SPACE FOR STABILIZATION
amorphous bridge to connect layers

MOIRÉ FAÇADE
22-02-2006

IMAGINED BY Daan Rietbergen
KEYWORDS layered construction, free form, sun shading, adaptable, envelope, 0-10 years, smart material

An array of tiles shifts over each other in order to block or let in sunlight. Each tile reacts to the sunlight individually. When this system is used on a curved surface, all tiles receive a different amount of sunlight, making every tile shift differently and thus creating a Moiré effect. The shifting process could be accomplished with a bi-metal, or other materials that react directly to the light. The tiles could be made of PV cells activating the bi-metal.

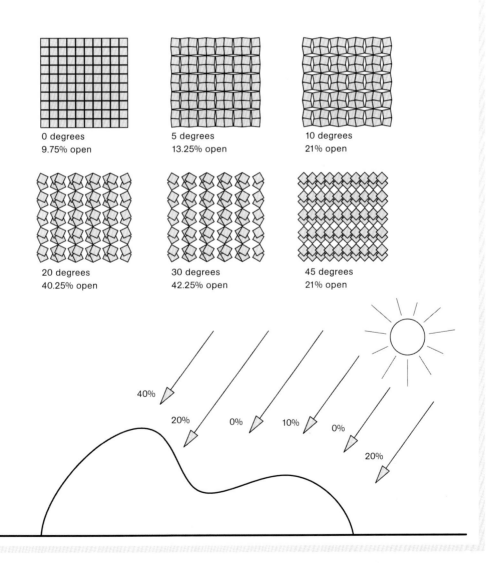

ELECTROSTATIC DUST FAÇADE
10-04-2006

IMAGINED BY Marcel Bilow
KEYWORDS sun-shading, transparency, low cost, organic

The idea is to collect the pollution / dust of the surrounding environment by means of an electrostatic load, meaning you can create free sun-shading devices, because dust is everywhere and free…. When you cut the power, the dust is blown or washed away by wind or rain. Based on a concept by R&Sie.

HOW ARE YOU TODAY?
11-05-2006

IMAGINED BY Linda Hildebrand
SUPPORTED BY Ulrich Knaack, Marcel Bilow
KEYWORDS temperature, light, thermochrome plastics

Mood rings change their color with different temperatures. The thermochrome plastic material, inserted instead of a jewel, changes its molecular structure with temperature differences, and breaks the light in different colors. If thermochrome pigments are added to the plastic material, that material can change its color reversibly or irreversibly. Used in a façade, the exterior could show which rooms are heated or which are currently exposed to solar irradiation.

BIO HEAT
22-05-2006

IMAGINED BY Linda Hildebrand
SUPPORTED BY Ulrich Knaack, Marcel Bilow
KEYWORDS bio-heat

In early spring, snowdrops grow through the snow covering the earth. This is possible, because they release energy in form of warmth. This biological warmth is about 8-10°C and is generated by burning glucose. A protective film protects the flowers from dehydration and cold. The analogy in a façade could be two layers with chemicals reacting with each other and releasing warmth in the space between the layers.

APPENDIX

CVs

ULRICH KNAACK (*1964) was trained as an architect at the RWTH Aachen, where he subsequently obtained his PhD in the field of structural use of glass. In subsequent years, he worked as an architect and general planner with RKW Architektur und Städtebau, Düsseldorf, winning several national and international competitions. His projects include high-rise buildings and stadiums. Today, he is Professor for Design and Building Technology at the Delft University of Technology, Netherlands, where he established the Façade Research Group and is also responsible for the Industrial Building Education research unit. He organized interdisciplinary design workshops such as the High-rise XXL. Knaack is also Professor for Design and Construction at the Detmolder Schule für Architektur und Innenarchitektur, Germany, and author of several well-known reference books.

TILLMANN KLEIN (*1967) studied architecture at the RWTH Aachen, completing his studies in 1994. He subsequently worked in several architectural offices; from 1996 onward he was employed by Gödde Architekten, focusing on the construction of metal and glass façades and glass roofs. At the same time, he attended the Kunstakademie in Düsseldorf, Klasse Baukunst, completing the studies in 2000 with the title "Meisterschüler". In 1999, he was co-founder of the architectural office rheinflügel baukunst with a focus on art-related projects. His practical work includes the design of a mobile museum for the Kunsthaus Zug, Switzerland, the design and construction of the façades for the ComIn Business Centre, Essen, project management for the construction of the Alanus Kunsthochschule, Bonn, project management for the extension of the University of Applied Sciences, Detmold. In 2005, he taught building construction at the Alanus Kunsthochschule, Bonn-Alfter. The same year, he was awarded the art prize of Nordrhein-Westphalen for young artists. Since September 2005 he has led the Façade Research Group at the TU Delft, Faculty of Architecture.

MARCEL BILOW (*1976) studied architecture at the University of Applied Science in Detmold, completing his studies with with honors in 2004. During this time, he also worked in several architectural offices, focusing on competitions and later on façade planning. Simultaneously, he and Fabian Rabsch founded the "raum204" architectural office. After graduating, he worked as a docent and became leader of research and development at the Chair for Design and Constructions at the FH Lippe & Höxter in Detmold under the supervision of Prof. Dr Ulrich Knaack. Since 2005, he has been member of the Façade Research Group at the TU Delft, Faculty of Architecture.

LIDIA BADARNAH (*1980) has a degree in architecture. Since December 2006 she has been working on her PhD in the department of Building Technology at Delft University of Technology. She studied at the Faculty of Architecture and Town Planning at the Technion-Israel Institute of Technology (Cum Laude). After graduation in 2005, she practised architecture at A Toledano Architects & Town Planning in Haifa, at Geurst & Schulze architecten bv in The Hague and at ONL (Oosterhuis_Lénárd) in Rotterdam. She was involved in housing, urban and public projects. Her work has been published in local Israeli magazines and newspapers. In 2005 she received the Reiskin Award for her graduation project.

ARIE BERGSMA (*1971) studied aerospace engineering at Delft University of Technology. After graduation in 1995, he worked as materials researcher at Hoogovens R&D, Product Application Centre (now TATA steel). From 1998 until 2004, he studied architecture and building technology at Eindhoven University. Before and during this period of part-time study, he worked at several engineering offices in the Netherlands: Prince Cladding BV, D3BN Structural Engineers and Peutz Consulting Engineers. At this last office, he worked as a consultant on building physics and acoustics from 2001 until 2006, and was involved in several large-scale building projects in the Netherlands (head offices of Shell and Hydron, Municipal Archives Amsterdam, Montevideo high-rise tower Rotterdam, Spuimarkt The Hague etc.). Since 2006, his activities have focused on research (as part-time researcher at the TU Delft) and consulting activities and projects with his own architectural office GAAGA.

THIEMO EBBERT (*1977) studied architecture at RWTH Aachen University and ETSAV Technical University St. Cugat in Barcelona after a professional education as technical craftsman at RKW Architektur und Städtebau in Düsseldorf (RKW), graduating in 2005. He gained professional experience in the design and realization of large-scale projects and façades again at RKW Architects, Düsseldorf, and DU Diederichs Project Management, Wuppertal, Germany (Space Park Bremen, German Stock Exchange, Frankfurt). Since September 2005, he haas been working as a researcher and tutor at the Faculty of Architecture, Chair of Design of Constructions at Delft Technical University, The Netherlands, focusing on systemized façade refurbishment.

DAAN RIETBERGEN (*1976) obtained his master degree in building technology at Delft University of Technology, after a bachelor study in architecture at the University for Professional Education in Amsterdam. He completed his master degree in 2003 in the Blob Technology Group on the topic of blob design and wind flow. He gained professional experience in designing and engineering free form interior and exterior projects at Vizona, Amsterdam (Orange-shops & I-Mode concept store) and the architecture office GROUP A in Rotterdam (Sabic European Headquarters). In November 2005 he commenced his work as a PhD candidate at the Faculty of Architecture at Delft University of Technology, the Netherlands. His research in the chair of Design of Constructions as well as the chair of Product Development focuses on the topic of Free Form Cladding Manufacturing.

REFERENCES

Ashby Shercliff et al.: *Materials – engineering, science, processing and design*, Butterworth Heinemann, Oxford 2007

Behnisch Architects, Transsolar ClimateEngineering: *Ecology.Design.Synergy*, Berlin 2006

Andrea Compagno: *Intelligente Glasfassaden – Material, Anwendung, Gestaltung*, Birkhäuser Verlag, Basle, 5. Auflage 2002

Klaus Daniels: *Gebäudetechnik – Ein Leitfaden für Architekten und Ingenieure*, Oldenbourg Verlag, Munich 1996

Klaus Daniels, Dirk U. Hindrichs: *Plusminus 20/40 Latitude - Sustainable Building Design in Tropical and Subtropical Regions*, Edition Axel Menges, Stuttgart 2002

Mike Davies: *A Wall for All Seasons*, in: *RIBA Journal*, 1981, Bd. 88, No. 2. – Deutsch: „Eine Wand für alle Jahreszeiten", in: *Arch+*, No. 104, 1990

Gerhard Hausladen, Michael de Saldanha, Petra Liedl, Christina Sager: *Clima Design – Lösungen für Gebäude, die mit weniger Technik mehr können*, Callwey Verlag, Munich 2005

Gerhard Hausladen, Michael de Saldanha, Petra Liedl: *Clima Skin – Konzepte für Gebäudehüllen, die mit weniger Energie mehr leisten*, Callwey Verlag, Munich 2006

Thomas Herzog, Roland Krippner, Werner Lang: *Fassaden Atlas*, Birkhäuser Verlag, Basle and Edition Detail, Munich 2004

Ulrich Knaack: *Konstruktiver Glasbau*, Rudolf Müller Verlag, Cologne 1998

Ulrich Knaack, Wilfried Führer, Jan Wurm: *Konstruktiver Glasbau 2*, Rudolf Müller Verlag, Cologne 2000

Ulrich Knaack, Tillmann Klein, Marcel Bilow, Thomas Auer: *Principles of Construction – Façades*, Birkhäuser Verlag, Berlin 2007

Christian Schittich (Hrsg.): *Gebäudehüllen – Konzepte, Schichten, Material*, Birkhäuser Verlag, Basle and Edition Detail, Munich 2001

Alex Steffen, et al.: *World Changing – a user's guide for the 21st century*, Harry N. Abrams, Inc., New York 2006

Eberhard Oesterle, Rolf-Dieter Lieb, Martin Lutz: *Doppelschalige Fassaden*, Callwey Verlag, Munich 1999

Frei Otto und Andere: *Natürliche Konstruktionen*, Stuttgart 1982

Uta Pottgiesser: *Fassadenschichtungen Glas*, Bauwerk Verlag, Berlin, 2004

Axel Ritter: *Smart Materials in Architektur, Innenarchitektur und Design*, Birkhäuser Verlag, Basle 2006

Andrew Watts: *Moderne Baukonstruktionen Fassaden*, Springer, Vienna 2004

Els Zijlstra: *Material Skills – Evolution of Materials*, Materia, Rotterdam 2005

CREDITS

IMAGINE

Series on technology and material development, Chair of Design of Constructions at Delft University of Technology. Imagine provides architects and designers with ideas and new possibilities for materials, constructions and façades by employing alternative or new technologies. It covers topics geared toward technical developments, environmental needs and aesthetic possibilities.

SERIES EDITORS
Ulrich Knaack, Tillman Klein, Marcel Bilow

PEER REVIEW
Prof. Dr Alan Brookes, Goring on Thames
Prof. Dr Gerhard Hausladen, Munich University of Technology
Prof. Kees Kaan, Delft University of Technology

FAÇADES

AUTHORS
Marcel Bilow, Tillman Klein, Ulrich Knaack

TEXT EDITING
Usch Engelmann, Linda Hildebrand, George Hall

DESIGN
Minke Themans

PRINTED BY
Die Keure, Brugge

ILLUSTRATION CREDITS
All illustrations by the authors and people who contributed to this book

©2008 010 Publishers, Rotterdam
www.010publishers.nl

ISBN 978-90-6450-656-7

ALSO PUBLISHED
Imagine 02
Deflateables
ISBN 978 90 6450 657 4

TO BE PUBLISHED
Imagine 03
Performance Driven Envelopes

Imagine 04
Rapids